MW00876697

HEALTHY COMMUNICATION WITH YOUR PARTNER

DISCOVER THE BENEFITS OF COMMUNICATING WITH EMOTIONAL INTELLIGENCE, EMPATHY & EFFECTIVE LISTENING SKILLS TO TURN CONFLICT INTO CONNECTION

AMANDA THOMAS

Copyright © 2023 Amanda Thomas. All rights reserved.

The content within this book may not be reproduced, duplicated, or transmitted without direct written permission from the author or the publisher.

Under no circumstances will any blame or legal responsibility be held against the publisher, or author, for any damages, reparation, or monetary loss due to the information contained within this book, either directly or indirectly.

Legal Notice:

This book is copyright protected. It is only for personal use. You cannot amend, distribute, sell, use, quote, or paraphrase any part of the content within this book, without the consent of the author or publisher.

Disclaimer Notice:

Please note the information contained within this document is for educational and entertainment purposes only. All effort has been expended to present accurate, up-to-date, reliable, and complete information. No warranties of any kind are declared or implied. Readers acknowledge that the author is not engaged in the rendering of legal, financial, medical, or professional advice. The content within this book has been derived from various sources. Please consult a licensed professional before attempting any techniques outlined in this book.

By reading this document, the reader agrees that under no circumstances is the author responsible for any losses, direct or indirect, that are incurred as a result of the use of the information contained within this document, including, but not limited to, errors, omissions, or inaccuracies.

CONTENTS

INTRODUCTION

"In a healthy relationship, communication is about sharing and understanding, not about winning and losing."

— ANONYMOUS

About two years into our marriage ...

I tried to keep it in. I closed my eyes and counted to ten as I breathed deeply. But when I opened my eyes, the pile of dirty dishes on the sink still made me see red. I pivoted, walked to the living room, where my husband was watching something on TV, and I blurted out ...

"Really?! Can't you even take care of your own dirty dishes? You open the dishwasher door and put stuff in it. That's how that works! Dishes do not magically go inside them!"

"I'll get to it."

"You'll get to it? When? When the kids are all grown up?"

"Okay, I'll do it now. I just had a really long day ..."

"STOP! Do not use that excuse. We both have full-time jobs, and somehow I manage to plan meals, do the groceries, cook dinner, and get the kids fed. You come home and feed yourself and cannot even put the dishes in the dishwasher!"

"I said okay, I'll ..."

"God, you exhaust me, Greg! You know this annoys me, but you never listen. You don't change because you don't care. You take me for granted and wait around until I pick up after you!"

I do not know what Greg said afterward. I honestly don't even remember if he said anything. After my speech, I whirled around, returned to the kitchen, and angrily shoved *his* dirty dishes in the dishwasher. I also wish I could tell you that this was an isolated incident. Sadly, it was not. I have had many such moments with Greg and him with me.

One time, we had an important dinner with his boss to attend. I was late getting ready, and he gave me the silent treatment while driving.

"I said I was sorry."

"Okay."

"But clearly you are not, so why don't you just say you're mad if you're mad."

"Fine! I'm mad. This dinner is important to me, and it's been on our schedule for a month."

"So?"

"So, you are sabotaging it."

"What?!"

"You are not supportive because this dinner is about me, not you."

As you can imagine, that night did not go well.

Greg and I would be like this for years, and with each conflict, we grew further and further apart. One night, the house was eerily quiet. Our eldest was in his early teens and having a sleepover with friends, while our youngest was in her room sleeping. Greg was in the living room watching something, and I sat beside him on the couch. We were both quiet. It hit me that it was not the comfortable silence shared by a happy, loving couple. It was the uneasy, awkward silence between two people who really had nothing to say to each other.

On our 15th wedding anniversary, Greg and I were goaded into having a big party to mark this milestone. I was alone in the bedroom, trying to list everything that needed to be prepared for the party when I noticed a heaviness in my heart. Tears started to fall, and I kept angrily wiping them away. (*I don't have time for this!*)

Greg suddenly opened the bedroom door, froze as he saw me, and did something unusual. He slowly closed the door behind him, walked towards me, sat at the edge of the bed to face me, and asked, *"What's wrong, Amanda?"* The gentleness in his voice, which I had not heard in a long time, undid me. I cried big fat tears and said:

"I don't want to have a 15ᵗʰ wedding anniversary party."

"Me either."

"I don't feel like celebrating because there's nothing to celebrate. But I still want "us" to work. Do you?"

Greg's voice broke a bit as he said, "More than anything."

"I think we need help."

"Okay. Let's get help."

I was filled with hope when Greg agreed. Once, I managed to drag Greg to a marriage counseling session, but it ended up as one big bust. For the first half of the session, neither of us wanted to talk; for the second half, we could not stop interrupting each other. We left the appointment angrier and more frustrated with each other. Since then, we have not sought any professional help.

Over the years, I had also probably bought every relationship self-help book I could access, and a few tips did help. Still, we always reverted back to our old ways of bickering and arguing with each other.

However, this time would be different. We both sensed that our relationship was hanging on by a thin thread, and we knew we needed to work together to save our marriage.

The following day, I called everyone to cancel our anniversary party plans and put all my energy into finding a marriage counselor. I think it was during our third or fourth session that we really started to dig into our relationship problems.

The counselor asked us NOT to interrupt each other; we would get our chance to speak. He also asked us NOT to look at each other as the other spoke; we were to simply absorb. With those two "house rules," he asked us to recall an argument, and I related the "dishwasher fight." At the end of my story, he asked:

"So what was the fight about?"

"I just said it; he doesn't put his dirty dishes in the dishwasher."

"Okay, but what was it REALLY about? What did those dirty dishes represent to you?"

"Ah, I guess they represented that he always leaves it up to me to take care of things."

"Okay, good. Now, Greg, do you remember the "dishwasher fight?"

"Yes."

"What was the fight about to you?"

"Dirty dishes in the sink."

"Okay, but what did those dirty dishes represent to you?"

"Dirty dishes in the sink."

In short, Greg and I discovered that we often viewed our problems from two different angles. We often jumped to conclusions and expected the worst from each other. We also blamed each other so often and hard that we didn't notice that we were burying our relationship deeper and deeper in trouble.

Blame was something we had never truly addressed before in our relationship. All the books and relationship advice I had seen before focused more on our expectations and how to get them. We did not fully address blaming, which was ironic as it was our "go-to" move.

Blame intensified the conflict in our relationship, so to repair our relationship, we needed to replace it with a more positive and effective way of communicating with each other. We also needed to stop trying to change each other and take more responsibility for our own thoughts, emotions, and behaviors in the relationship.

I am not going to lie to you. It takes A LOT of time and effort to unlearn damaging and unhealthy communication habits and learn new, effective ways of communicating with your partner. The counseling sessions we attended jump-started the change for us. Still, it would take time, a bookshelf worth of relationship self-help books, countless relationship forums, and various advice from couples we admired and respected to get our relationship back on track.

But here is what I can promise you: There is hope! A happy and emotionally stable relationship is possible if you are both committed to the process. Greg and I were, and our relationship is as happy and strong as ever. (We just celebrated our 25th wedding anniversary!)

When Greg and I started this journey to fix our relationship, our goal was, quite honestly, to stop fighting all the time. Our arguments were zapping our energies and spirit, and we were exhausted and miserable.

As we discovered new ways of communicating and resolving our conflicts, we were surprised at how much EVERYTHING improved. As our fights lessened, we became closer to each other. A level of trust and openness that was never there before emerged between us. Even things in the bedroom started to improve drastically.

Soon enough, family and friends noticed our positive changes and asked questions.

What's the secret to a happy marriage?

How do you become "in tune" with each other?

How do you handle problems?

What do you do when you're exasperated with each other?

What do you do to get your partner to listen?

What do you do to get your partner to help?

What do you do when you disagree with each other?

I'm ready to give up. Is there still hope?

I am always willing to answer such questions because I remember how close Greg and I came to losing each other. I remember how unhappy we were and how desperately we needed help. So, I understand you, dear reader, because I was you.

How did we do it? How did we go from fighting to loving and supporting each other again? As I said, it was a very long journey but one that I am more than willing to share with you. This book is the culmination of all I have learned in the past 25 years of marriage. In the following pages, you will:

- Discover the #1 reason why we blame and the #1 reason why we should not do it.
- Find out what you must do (step-by-step) to stop blaming and attacking each other.
- Learn your communication style and how you can use this knowledge to prevent misunderstandings and arguments.

- Realize that what you DON'T SAY can be more powerful and damaging than the words you use in conversations.
- Understand the importance of empathy to connect with your partner.
- Get practical tips and strategies to increase your emotional intelligence (EQ), which improves your communication skills. (It's easier than you think.)
- Discover how to accept personal responsibility for your emotions, thoughts, and actions in your relationship. (It's harder than you think.)
- Learn how to expertly handle even the most difficult conversations (blame-free conflict resolution).
- Find out why patience is as vital as love in relationships. (And more importantly, learn how to develop more patience!)
- Know how to rebuild trust and safety in your relationship. (Most people get this wrong!)
- Discover how to maintain healthy communication in the long term.

Important: You will find more than general theories as you go through the above information. Most of the relationship advice I read about or was given in the past was vague. I was never given the specifics on HOW to actually make changes in our relationship. So I made certain that this book contains realistic, step-by-step, doable techniques that you can use to put what you learn into practice.

During the "dark years" of our relationship, there were times when it felt like we were drowning. And when we finally started slowly figuring out what works, we often said aloud, *"If only someone gave us good, real-life advice on how to do this!"*

I hope, dear reader, you will let ME be that *someone* for you.

If you are tired of fighting and shedding tears, fed up with all the conflict, and want to stop feeling alone in your relationship ...

If you want to discover how to communicate effectively, connect with your partner and make your relationship work ...

Then please turn the page and keep on reading till the end.

To less conflict and more connection,

Amanda Thomas

Happy Wife and Mother

1

THE BLAME GAME

"You do not blame your shadow for the shape of your body. Just the same: Do not blame others for the shape of your experience."

— *GILLIAN DUCE*

When faced with conflict in our relationships, we often fight and blame each other. And we resort to blaming because we believe that our partners are not living up to our expectations. It does not matter if we contributed to the situation. In our minds, the other person is to blame. But why do we think the other person is wrong, bad, or less? Part of the reason is where most relationships start—dating.

DATING = GREAT EXPECTATIONS

When we date, we put our best foot forward. And that is perfectly normal. After all, no one gets a second chance at making a great first impression.

Ideally, as the dating phase progresses, we start to truly know each other. We look at each other, see both positive and negative sides (after all, NO ONE is perfect), and still fall in love and decide to have a relationship. Unfortunately, in many cases, in our attempts to impress each other, we may not be showing our authentic selves.

So, instead of falling in love with each other's real version, we fall in love with each other's best performance. From there, we decide to be together, make plans, and have great expectations about our future.

However, no one is perfect, and sooner or later, we WILL reveal ourselves in our entirety—warts and all. You or your partner (or both) are now disappointed. The big reveal has occurred, and you realize that the person you are with may not be that amazing after all.

Faced with this imperfection, you become disillusioned and disappointed. At this stage, the following usually happens.

1. You blame your partner for your unhappiness.
2. You judge your partner's behavior as wrong, unfair, or unjust.

3. You try to change your partner.
4. Your partner feels attacked and becomes withdrawn or defensive.
5. You and your partner become emotionally disconnected, and the relationship deteriorates.

You become so busy with steps 1 to 3 above that you miss something crucial: your contribution to the problem. Yes, we often fail to realize how our emotions, thoughts, and actions contribute to the occurrence and persistence of our relationship problems.

But first, what exactly is *blame*, and why do we do it in our relationships?

WHAT IS BLAME?

Blame is an assessment of a person's (in this case, your partner's) behavior as morally or socially wrong.[1] According to psychologists, blame usually has three main components:

- the behavior being analyzed
- assessing whether the behavior caused the negative consequence
- assessing whether the person who behaved that way intended to do so[2]

When you blame your partner, you pick their specific behavior, judge it as bad or wrong, and take it to mean that they did it on purpose!

WHY WE BLAME...

Disillusionment. Disappointment. Anger. Pain. Hurt. Loneliness. Despair. Emptiness. Hopelessness. Sadness.

These are all intense emotions to experience in a relationship. When these emotions become too much to bear, it is easy to resort to blame. You see, **blaming is a defense mechanism**. It helps us maintain our self-esteem by allowing us to avoid awareness of our own imperfections or shortcomings. But here is the problem: When we blame, we shift responsibility. We surrender ownership of our feelings and contributions in a situation.

It is said that being mad (showing anger) is easier than being sad (admitting hurt or pain). Similarly, blaming (pointing fingers) is easier than feeling shame (admitting wrongdoing).

So, the **biggest (or main) reason we blame our partners is that we do not want or do not know how to take responsibility for our part in creating problems in our relationships**.

Here are some other reasons why we blame our partners.

1. **Blame is a means to share or shift the pain.** We reach the blaming stage because we are unhappy in our relationships and want our partners to feel that misery too. So, we resort to blaming to try and hurt them.

2. **Blame makes us feel right and powerful.** Humans hate being wrong and admitting mistakes.[3,4] As a result, when we experience conflict or problems in our relationships that make us miserable, we tend to look elsewhere as the cause of the problem.

3. **Blame is a way to get attention.** This speaks of a *victim mindset*, which is a way of thinking where a person considers themselves a victim of circumstances or the acts of others. In this context, blame is not a way to gain power but rather an admission of powerlessness.

4. **We blame because this is what we know**. Some studies show that blaming can be a learned behavior. [5,6] If we grew up in an environment where blaming was the norm, we may be more likely to resort to this behavior in our relationships.

Important: Blame has nothing to do with who may or may not be causing the problem(s) in the relationship. It is refusing to face and accept one's responsibilities in the relationship. It is an unwillingness to be part of the solution.

So, now that you know what blaming is and why you or your partner might be doing it, it is time to learn why blaming is NOT the answer to your relationship problems.

AND WHY WE SHOULDN'T

The **#1 reason we should not blame in relationships is this: It does not solve anything**! In fact, it makes things worse.

Imagine being trapped in a maze. Whenever we blame, the maze gets bigger and more complicated—but no one gets out. Blaming is like constantly trapping your relationship in a maze of problems and pain.

Here are some other reasons why blaming your partner negatively impacts your relationship.

1. **Blaming is subjective.** When evaluating your partner's behavior, you subject their thoughts, feelings, and emotions to *your* moral code. This can damage relationships because it creates an atmosphere of defensiveness and anger. The one being blamed may resort to thoughts such as, *Who made you the boss; Who made you the judge of right and wrong;* or *What right do you have to judge me as "less?*

2. **Blame does not listen and creates a culture of fear.** A person who blames has already judged the other person to be at fault. The blamer's mind is already

made up and closed, so there is not much point in hearing the other person out. When this happens, we create a culture of fear where the ones being blamed may be afraid to express themselves and be vulnerable.

3. **Constant blaming is a form of emotional abuse.** Being blamed for something repeatedly is like taking a verbal beating. Even if the person being accused is the cause of the conflict, getting blamed all the time is not productive. It builds resentment and damages the emotional safety of your relationship.

4. **Blaming can be a form of gaslighting.** Gaslighting is when someone makes another feel accountable for something they may not have done or caused. The blamer may be trying to manipulate the other person's perception of reality, making their partner doubt themselves. This can be especially harmful if the partner begins to internalize the blame and believe they are at fault, even when they are not. Over time, this can erode their self-esteem and make them more vulnerable to emotional abuse.

5. **Blaming reduces intimacy.** Understandably, feeling close and intimate with someone who constantly points fingers and assumes the worst in you is difficult. The person being blamed may keep their distance as they develop bitter feelings towards their partner. If the accuser is basing their blame on lies to avoid responsibility, they, too, may

step away from their partner to keep their sense of self-worth.

6. **Blaming ignores the bigger picture.** Blaming focuses on individual actions and behaviors rather than the underlying issues causing the relationship problems. By focusing on blame, we are essentially missing the forest for the trees and preventing ourselves from addressing the root causes of our problems.

All in all, **blaming is a toxic way of dealing with relationship problems**. When we blame, we tell our partners, *"This is your fault—fix it,"* and that we are unwilling to work together to solve our problems.

Please remember that **a relationship should be Me + You rather than Me vs. You**. So, it does not matter who is at fault. What matters is working together to find a solution to the problem.

So, now that you know that blaming harms relationships, how do you stop doing it?

TOP 7 TIPS TO STOP PLAYING THE BLAME GAME

Blaming is a behavior that you can unlearn. Here are some tips to stop playing the blame game.

1. Be aware of when you resort to blaming tactics. One of the most tell-tale signs of blaming is when someone starts their sentences with "**You**."

"You never think of me."

"You always do this."

"You should not have done that."

"You never listen."

"You always pass things to me."

"You never help with dinner."

Notice, too, that the above are absolute statements. There is no room for doubt, explanations, or even arguments.

What should you do instead? Start sentences with "I," and then express how you feel instead of labeling or judging your partner's actions.

NOT: "You never think of me."

But This, Instead: "I feel forgotten and ignored when ..."

NOT: "You always do this."

But This Instead: "I feel upset when [x] happens repeatedly."

NOT: "You should not have done that."

But This, Instead: "I would prefer if we could handle this situation differently in the future because ..."

NOT: "You never listen."

But This, Instead: "I feel disregarded when ... or I feel like I'm not being heard when ..."

NOT: "You always pass things to me."

But This, Instead: "I feel overwhelmed when ..."

NOT: "You never help with dinner."

But This, Instead: "I need help with dinner. Can you please help?"

Let us take a moment to examine this last example. Did you notice these major differences?

YOU vs. I	
You never help with dinner.	*I need help with dinner. Can you please help?*
Focus: partner	Focus: self
Judgmental	Non-judgmental; not accusatory
Closed mentality; absolute	Open mentality; asking for opinion; open to discussion
Provokes defensiveness, anger	Induces collaboration
Adds to conflict	Aims to resolve conflict

WORKSHEET: I

Moving from "You" to "I" takes practice. Check out the **"I" Worksheet** in Appendix A to start making it a habit.

2. Take a break when needed. Discussions can easily escalate to arguments and arguments to blaming. If you feel overwhelmed or frustrated or notice your partner getting so, take a break from the conversation and return to it when you are both calm.

3. Practice more empathy and less judgment. Instead of applying the *"You are wrong"* mentality, ask, *"Why did they do that?"* instead. By shifting your mindset to trying to understand your partner, kindness wins in your relationship.

4. Practice the 50/50 rule. Life does not just happen to you, and your relationship is not the sole responsibility of your partner. So, when problems arise, ask yourself questions such as:

"What was my role in this?"

"Why am I reacting this way?"

"What can I do to make things better?"

Introspection will help you more accurately identify where the problem is coming from and prevent you from projecting your issues onto your partner.

5. Forgive. Blame fosters negative emotions from both parties. Holding on to grudges only fuels the conflict. It is better to practice forgiveness.

WORKSHEET: Forgiveness

Do you find it hard to forgive? If so, check out the **How to Forgive Worksheet** in Appendix A.

---

6. Concentrate on the problem, not your partner. When emotions are high, it is easy to start looking at your partner with daggers in your eyes. Avoid this by focusing on the issue or the problem at hand. Stay true to the topic and avoid personal attacks.

7. Focus on finding solutions. Blaming is going backward instead of forward. It focuses on who you think is the cause of the problem instead of trying to solve it. Instead of pointing fingers, work together to find solutions that address the underlying problems. This can involve brainstorming ideas, compromising, and making concrete plans to implement changes.

Playing the blame game leads to resentment, anger, and distance between two people in a relationship. It is also an "outward" approach (i.e., looking at others). So, why not apply an "inward" approach instead of doing that? That is, divert your attention to yourself and take responsibility for your emotions and behaviors in your relationship.

IT STARTS WITH YOU: STOP BLAMING; START OWNING

Even though you are in a relationship, you are your own person. No one should be responsible for your emotions, thoughts, and actions but you. Taking responsibility for your emotions and behaviors in relationships is essential for several reasons.

First, it allows you to **maintain control over your own life**. Taking responsibility for your feelings and reactions makes you less likely to feel like a victim or become overwhelmed by negative emotions.

Second, taking responsibility helps you **build healthier relationships**. Blaming creates resentment and defensiveness in your partner. By taking ownership of your feelings and actions, you demonstrate maturity and respect for your partner's feelings, which can help foster a more positive and loving relationship.

Additionally, it helps you to **communicate more effectively**. When you are not blaming and are in tune with your own feelings and actions, you can better express your needs and desires clearly and respectfully. This clarity can help prevent misunderstandings and conflict, promoting greater understanding and closeness in your relationship.

Finally, taking responsibility helps you **develop greater self-awareness and personal growth**. By reflecting on your thoughts and feelings and taking ownership of your actions, you can better understand yourself and your behavior patterns. This understanding can help you to make positive changes and to grow as a person, which can benefit not only your relationship but also your overall well-being.

So, what does taking responsibility look like?

1. **Be honest with yourself.** It is easy to pass blame (focus: others) and difficult to admit mistakes (focus: self). However, being dishonest with yourself can lead to self-deception, self-sabotage, and a lack of personal growth. It also harms your relationship because you cannot form a genuine connection with your partner. You can do several things to practice being more honest with yourself: practice self-reflection, keep a journal, practice mindfulness, ask for feedback from others, etc.

2. **Do not be defensive.** Be aware of defensive responses like *"Stop being so dramatic,"* *"How am I supposed to know what you are thinking,"* or *"You should have said something sooner."* Remember, focus inwards first.

3. **Apologize if necessary.** If you realize you have made a mistake, apologize. Sticking to your guns despite knowing you are or may be at fault is your ego at work. Further, it just prolongs the conflict. If your partner is apologizing, be gracious, accept the apology, and move on. Do not accept the apology

and then antagonize by saying something like, *"That's okay ... I hope you know better next time."*

Important: Remember that you should only take responsibility for YOUR emotions, thoughts, and behavior. If your partner blames you for something that has nothing to do with you, do not take responsibility. Sometimes, just going along with it to move on from the situation may seem fine. However, in the long run, it might lead to unhealthy behaviors in you and your partner.

Blaming is not unusual in relationships, but it is harmful. So, if you want to repair your relationship, you need to **STOP** blaming and **START** learning new ways to communicate with each other. If you think that is easier said than done, you are right. Luckily, the following pages will help you achieve just that.

2

HOW TO "SPEAK" TO IMPROVE YOUR RELATIONSHIP

"To effectively communicate, we must realize that we are all different in the way we perceive the world and use this understanding as a guide to our communication with others."

— *TONY ROBBINS*

Do you ever feel like, no matter how hard you try to explain your point of view, you and your partner always seem to be on different pages when there is a disagreement? It is like speaking two separate languages! But before you get frustrated, consider the possibility that it is not WHAT you are saying but HOW you and your partner are communicating.

Our *communication style* refers to how we connect and converse with others. It involves not only the words we use while speaking but also the tone, language, and nonverbal cues we use. Many factors, such as your personality, childhood, cultural background, gender, age, etc, influence your communication style.

Knowing your and your partner's communication styles is crucial to avoid misunderstandings, headaches, and heartaches. Note that you DO NOT have to have the same communication style to connect effectively, but you do have to know each other's style to understand each other better.

According to experts, there are five (5) communication styles. Here's a quick rundown of each of them. Can you tell which one fits you?

THE FIVE COMMUNICATION STYLES

Passive Communication

Passive communication is a style in which people evade conveying their thoughts or needs. They often give in to the needs of others and go along with things even if they disagree. For this reason, this style is also known as the *submissive* communication style. Some of the nonverbal cues of passive communicators are avoiding eye contact and having poor posture. People who communicate passively may fear conflict or rejection and, as a result, do not express their true feelings or desires. The problem with this communication style is that it can lead to resentment and unmet needs in the long run.

Here are some examples of what people might say under this communication style:

"It's okay. You don't have to worry about it."

This can indicate that the person is uncomfortable expressing their needs or concerns and may be trying to avoid conflict.

"I don't know. What do you want to do?"

This may indicate that the person is uncomfortable expressing their preferences or opinions and prefer to rely on others.

"I'm fine, don't worry about me."

This statement may indicate that the person is uncomfortable expressing their emotions and may be trying to avoid appearing vulnerable.

"Whatever you want is fine with me."

This statement may indicate that the person is uncomfortable expressing their needs or opinions and may be trying to please the other person.

"I guess it's my fault."

This statement may indicate that the person is uncomfortable standing up for themselves and may be taking the blame to avoid conflict.

Aggressive Communication

Aggressive communication involves forcefully expressing opinions, needs, and desires without regard for others' feelings. Some of the nonverbal cues of aggressive communicators are speaking loudly and using dominant postures and gestures.

For example, a person who talks aggressively might stand up straight so they can deliberately look down at the person they are talking to. They may also use dominant gestures, such as wildly gesturing with their hands or blocking the other person's way. This communication style can often be hurtful and intimidating to others, leading to conflict and damaged relationships.

Here are some examples of what people with this communication style might say:

"You never listen to me! Why do I even bother talking to you?"

This statement is confrontational and accusatory, indicating a lack of respect for the other person's perspective.

"I don't care what you think; this is how it's going to be."

This statement dismisses the other person's opinions and can indicate a desire for control.

"You're always doing things wrong. I'll just do it myself."

This statement is critical and can indicate a lack of trust in the other person's abilities.

"What's wrong with you? Why can't you ever do anything right?"

This statement is demeaning and can indicate a lack of empathy or understanding for the other person's feelings.

"If you don't do what I say, there will be consequences."

This statement is threatening and can indicate a desire for power and control over another person.

Passive-Aggressive Communication

Passive-aggressive communication is a blend of both passive and aggressive communication styles. Individuals who communicate this way often use sarcasm, silence, passive resistance, irony, or other indirect means to express their needs or opinions. They also usually apply a sweet and innocent persona. As you can imagine, this style can lead to confusion, hurt feelings, and damage relationships.

Here are some examples of what people with this communication style might say:

"Oh, don't worry about me. I'll just stay here and finish all the work by myself."

This statement is a passive-aggressive way of expressing frustration about not receiving help from others and can indicate a desire for control.

"I'm not mad. It's fine. Do whatever you want."

This statement can indicate underlying anger or resentment.

"Sure, I'll do it. I guess I have nothing else to do anyway."

This statement may indicate a desire to punish or guilt the other person for not helping.

"I was just kidding. Can't you take a joke?"

This statement is a way of deflecting responsibility for a hurtful or disrespectful comment. It can be an indication of a lack of accountability.

"You're so lucky just to go out and have fun while I stay here and do all the work."

This passive-aggressive statement can indicate jealousy or resentment towards the other person.

Manipulative Communication Style

Manipulative communication involves trying to control or influence others to achieve a desired outcome, often at the expense of the other person's feelings or needs. Manipulative communicators are often insincere and bury their real intent beneath lies and deception. This communication style damages relationships because it erodes trust over time.

Here are some examples of what people with this communication style might say:

"I don't know. It's just something to think about."

This statement is vague and ambiguous—on purpose. It is meant to confuse others or leave them unsure of what the speaker really means or wants.

"I guess I'll just have to figure this out myself."

This statement uses guilt or shame to get others to do what the speaker wants.

"I'm just so overwhelmed! I don't know what to do."

This statement indicates that the speaker is pretending to be helpless or victimized to gain sympathy or support.

"You're the best! What will I ever do without you?"

This speaker is using false flattery or charm to win people over, gain their trust, and make them more likely to do what the speaker wants them to do next time.

Assertive Communication

Assertive communication is the most effective and respectful style of communication. Assertive communicators express their opinions, needs, and desires directly and honestly while respecting others. Some of the nonverbal cues of these communicators are using a balanced tone of voice and relaxed postures and gestures. This communication style is clear and effective, leading to healthy relationships.

Here are some examples of what people with this communication style might say:

"I hear and understand your perspective, honey, but I disagree."

This statement shows that the person acknowledges the other person's opinion while still expressing their own.

"I need your help with this task. Can you please assist me?"

This statement is clear and direct and expresses their need while respecting the other person's time and availability.

"I feel hurt when you speak to me in that tone. Can we discuss how we can communicate more respectfully?"

This statement expresses the person's feelings while suggesting a solution and encouraging dialogue.

"I appreciate your offer, but I have other commitments that I need to attend to."

This statement expresses the person's needs and boundaries while acknowledging the other person's offer.

"I apologize for any misunderstandings. Can we clarify what we both mean and work towards a resolution?"

This assertive statement expresses the person's desire for clarity and resolution while taking responsibility for misunderstandings.

QUIZ:

Do you know your communication style? If not and want to discover it, take the quick **Communication Style Self-Assessment Questionnaire** in Appendix A.

It's important to note that communication is not just done through words. In fact, what you do NOT say is often more revealing than what you do say.

NONVERBAL COMMUNICATION (A.K.A. TELL ME WHAT YOU REALLY THINK)

Nonverbal communication is communicating through gestures, facial expressions, body language, tone of voice, and other forms of communication that do not involve words. It's a way of conveying meaning and emotions without using language. In relationships, nonverbal cues can often be more powerful than the words you use.

For example, say your partner is anxious about speaking in front of a crowd. If you smile, nod, or give an enthusiastic thumbs up, you convey your love and support. You say, *"You got this!"* without using any words. On the other hand, if you smirk or frown, you ridicule your partner's feelings and effectively say, *"Really?!?"*

It's important to remember that nonverbal communication is often very telling because we do it unconsciously. Yes, nonverbal cues can be more honest than words. For example, say you asked your partner to come home early tonight, and they said *"Sure"* while looking away and leaving the room while you were still talking. Which one would you trust? The words or the actions? Of course, this goes both ways. You also communicate your true thoughts and emotions to your partner nonverbally.

If the nonverbal communication is positive, then it strengthens the relationship. But if it's negative, then it weakens and destroys it. Following are several different types of nonverbal communication and how to use them effectively to improve communication in your relationship.

1. Body Language: This includes posture, gestures, and facial expressions. Positive body language can show your partner that you are present, engaged, and interested in what they have to say. Positive body language includes:

- smiling
- maintaining eye contact
- standing up straight
- open and relaxed posture
- nodding or tilting the head to show interest
- leaning slightly towards the person speaking

- using open-hand gestures
- mirroring the other person's body language to show engagement and understanding
- making appropriate facial expressions that convey interest, empathy, or agreement
- touching or holding hands, if appropriate and comfortable for both partners

2. Tone of Voice: How you speak can convey a lot of information about your emotional state and the message you are attempting to relay. Using a positive tone of voice helps create a comfortable and supportive atmosphere in your relationship. This, in turn, encourages your partner to open up and express themselves more freely to you. A positive tone of voice can include the following:

- speaking in a warm and friendly manner
- using a calm and relaxed tone
- speaking clearly and at a moderate pace
- using a pleasant and cheerful tone
- using humor and light-heartedness when appropriate
- expressing empathy and understanding when discussing difficult topics
- using encouraging words and phrases like *"I believe in you!"* or *"You've got this."*

- using a confident tone when expressing your needs and opinions while respecting your partner's perspective

But what if I'm angry?

I met a couple who had been married for about 40 years a few years ago. When I asked how they handle arguments, they said something I'll never forget: *"When someone shouts, the conversation stops."*

With this simple remark, I realized Greg and I had been doing precisely that. We blamed and argued endlessly, but we were not having a genuine conversation. We talked *at* each other, not *with* each other. Since then, whenever I am annoyed or angry, I calm myself down before speaking with Greg.

3. Eye Contact: Making eye contact with your partner can help you establish a connection and convey interest and attention. It can also help you pick up on nonverbal cues and better understand what your partner is trying to communicate. Positive eye contact practices can include:

- Maintain eye contact when you're speaking to your partner to convey that you're interested in any answer, comments, or feedback they may have.
- Maintain eye contact when your partner is talking to show that you're actively listening and engaged in the conversation.

- Look into your partner's eyes during intimate moments to convey love and intimacy.
- Look into your partner's eyes when expressing gratitude or appreciation to show sincerity and depth of feeling.
- Maintain eye contact when discussing difficult topics to show that you're committed to resolving the issue and working through any challenges together.
- Use eye contact to convey empathy and understanding during moments of conflict, even if you disagree with your partner's perspective.
- When meeting your partner's family or friends, use eye contact to convey respect and interest in getting to know them better.
- During shared activities or experiences, use eye contact to convey a sense of connection and shared enjoyment.

4. Touch: Physical touch is a potent way of expressing love, affection, and support. It also helps reduce stress and promote connection and intimacy.[1] Positive touch communication can include:

- holding hands
- embracing/Hugging
- kissing, even a quick peck on the cheek
- cuddling/Snuggling
- giving each other massages

- holding each other
- a gentle, comforting pat on the back or shoulder

5. Proximity: The physical gap between you and your partner reveals much about your relationship. Being too close or far apart indicates your level of comfort and interest in each other. Furthermore, proximity "improves communication readiness." [2] So, the distance between you signifies whether or not your relationship's communication is healthy. Positive proximity can include:

- sitting close to each other
- holding hands while walking
- hugging, cuddling, or snuggling before sleeping
- standing close and facing each other during conversations
- leaning in and resting your head on your partner's shoulder
- sharing a blanket or coat to stay warm

TOP 5 COMMUNICATION MISTAKES IN RELATIONSHIPS

Suppose you and your partner have trouble understanding each other. In that case, frustration kicks in, and you will likely make communication mistakes in your relationship. What mistakes, you might wonder?

1. You do not actively listen to your partner. When your partner is speaking, give them your FULL attention. Do not start planning in your head what you want to say next. If you are not actively listening, you disregard their point of view, and doing so prevents you from understanding them.

WORKSHEET: Active Listening

When you are used to blaming, you are not used to listening. So how do you change this habit? Check out the **Active Listening Worksheet** in Appendix A.

2. You let your emotions do the talking. Do not allow your emotions to take over and dictate your language and behavior without taking the time to think things through or consider the consequences of your actions.

For example, saying, *"I can't believe you did that! How could you be so thoughtless and selfish? You always do this, and it's really starting to get on my nerves. I'm so sick of it!"* is expressing anger and frustration in an attacking and accusatory way. Instead, say, *"I feel hurt and frustrated about what happened. It's important that we consider each other's feelings and needs. Can we discuss how to work together to prevent this from happening again?"*

3. You assume your partner is a mind reader. One of the most common communication mistakes is assuming your partner knows precisely what you want. NO ONE can fully understand another person's thoughts and intentions, so to avoid misunderstandings, clearly say what you want or need from the situation.

4. You hide your true feelings to avoid conflict. Sometimes, you might want to give up on the conversation just to be done with it. For example, you might say, *"Okay. We're good,"* even though you are not just to avoid conflict. However, remember that this avoids discussing the problem and does not solve anything.

5. You adopt a "solving" instead of "listening" approach. Listen when your partner communicates problems or unpleasant emotions to you. There is no need "fix" the issue. Your partner is venting and wants to hear you support them; they do not need you to solve their problems. Of course, as a loving partner, you want to help, so say, *"How can I help you?"* or *"Is there anything I can do for you?"* Do not make plans to solve the issue without consulting them. Doing so disregards them and communicates that you think they cannot solve their own problems.

So far, you have learned about different communication styles, the importance of nonverbal cues, and the common communication mistakes people make in relationships. All these will help you effectively communicate your wants and needs to your partner. But what about their wants and needs?

How do you connect with your partner and truly understand what they need from you and your relationship? For this, you need to be *empathic*.

3

MASTERING EMPATHY IN COMMUNICATION

"Empathy is seeing with the eyes of another, listening with the ears of another, and feeling with the heart of another."

— *ALFRED ADLER*

People enter relationships for various reasons but, in general, we enter relationships because we want to connect with someone. We want to connect physically, mentally, and emotionally in a safe space (i.e., your relationship). **True connection begins with building empathy**.

Empathy is being able to understand and feel what your partner feels. It means trying to see things from their point of view while being aware of your own thoughts and reactions.

For example, say you have had a long day at work, and all you want to do is go home, hit the shower, and decompress. However, upon arriving, you see your partner doubled over on the couch from stomach flu. You suddenly feel the need to take care of them. You want to do what you can to make them feel better, and your focus shifts to them.

Empathy is crucial in a healthy and stable relationship for several reasons:

Connection: Empathy helps to create a deeper sense of connection and intimacy between partners. When we feel understood and heard, we are more likely to trust and open up to our partners, strengthening our bond.

Communication: Empathy is essential for effective communication. When we empathize with our partners, we can better understand their needs, desires, and concerns. Empathizing also means being able to speak with each either in respectful and compassionate ways.

Conflict Resolution: When we can see things from our partner's perspective, we can better find common ground and work together to find solutions to our relationship problems.

Emotional Support: Empathy allows us to provide emotional support to our partners during difficult times. By understanding their feelings and offering compassion and validation, we can help them feel heard and cared for.

Emotional Safety: When we show our partners understanding, care, and compassion, we create an emotionally safe relationship. Empathy tells our partners, *"I got you,"* and *"You are safe here."* This, in turn, will encourage them to do the same for us.

EMPATHIC LISTENING: I HEAR YOU

Empathy is a positive attitude you can cultivate. Here are some tips on how you can become a more empathic listener.

1. Be an active listener. As mentioned before, active listening is paying full attention to the speaker. Listen not only with your ears but also your eyes by noting their nonverbal cues (e.g., voice tone, body language, facial expressions, etc.). The ultimate goal in active listening is to fully comprehend the message your partner is trying to convey. (See also Worksheet: Active Listening.)

2. Be non-judgmental. Whatever your partner is saying, absorb it. Avoid jumping to conclusions or making assumptions about what they are saying. Instead, try to remain open-minded and listen with curiosity and interest.

3. Ask questions. Empathy is practicing a more profound sense of understanding. For example, when your partner says they had a rough day, do not just reply, *"Oh, okay."*

Respond by saying, *"Tell me more about what happened."* Open-ended questions such as this give your partner complete freedom to say whatever they want to express.

However, do not push. Do not force your partner to share anything they are not ready to share. The goal is not to nag but to allow your partner to share more.

If, on the other hand, the question makes them open up and share a lot, give them the time and space to do so. Let them control the conversation.

4. Show compassion and kindness. Suppose you cooked macaroni and cheese for dinner for the first time. However, instead of eating with gusto, your partner seems distant and barely touches their food. When you asked what was going on, they said they did not like macaroni and cheese at all. When asked, *"Can you tell me more why you feel this way?"* they said the meal reminds them of their unpleasant childhood.

Now, for you, it is the opposite. You love mac 'n cheese; it brings only fond childhood memories, but perhaps now is NOT the time to share them. Do not shift the focus to yourself. Instead, accept your partner's experience as different and show compassion and kindness.

5. Step into their shoes. Now is the time for reflection and gaining a deeper understanding of your partner. Using the mac n' cheese example above, suppose your partner elaborated that the meal brings back unhappy memories of poverty; mac 'n cheese in a box was all they ate for a time.

Based on what you learned, start to imagine how it must have been for your partner to grow up under those circumstances. Does it explain some of their current behavior regarding food, money, or eating habits?

Listening, comprehending, and seeing things from your partner's point of view—that is empathy.

EMPATHIC SPEAKING: I SEE YOU

If you watched the movie *Avatar*, you must have heard the phrase *"I see you"* in the movie. The Na'vi people use the phrase to greet and acknowledge another person's presence and inner spirit.

For the Na'vi, the phrase *"I see you"* represents a deeper level of seeing. It is not just about someone's physical presence; it implies recognizing the other person's inner, authentic self. *"I see you"* means I see who you are, I understand you, and I accept you.

Empathic listening is just part of the equation; how you respond is the other part. Here are examples of responses you might want to say when your partner shares a personal or unpleasant experience with you.

1. Celebrate their courage. Appreciate their bravery in being vulnerable with you. Express your gratitude that they decided to confide in you, and assure them that you will keep what they have disclosed confidential.

Example: *"Thank you for sharing this with me, honey. It must've been difficult, and it's important, so I know this stays between us."*

2. Connect with their emotions. During conversations, show you are listening not just to your partner's words but to what they are feeling.

Example: *"I know you're feeling really sad about this."*

3. Be their cheerleader. Boost your partner's morale by highlighting their strengths, which will help them overcome what they are going through—without diminishing their experience.

Example: *"I can't imagine how difficult this is, babe. But I know you've been through something similar, so I have complete faith you'll get through this too."*

4. Express concern and support. Assure your partner that you are there for them and want to help in any way they want.

Example: *"Is there anything I could do to make you feel better?"*

5. Check-in. After some time, ask your partner how they are doing. This shows your ongoing concern for their well-being.

Example: *"How are you today, babe? Let me know if you want to talk more about it or would like some space. Either way, I'm here."*

ASSERTIVE + EMPATHIC SPEAKING: HEAR AND SEE ME TOO

If you are the one who wants to speak or share something with your partner, the best way to (1) get your message across and (2) receive the response or feedback you want is to be an assertive and empathic speaker.

You want to be assertive because you don't want your wants and needs dismissed. However, no one wants to be blamed, dictated to, or feel threatened in a conversation. As such, you need to be empathic. Here are some tips on how to achieve this:

1. Take a moment. Find a quiet and comfortable place to sit and focus on your breath. (The more important or challenging the conversation, the more you need to do this.) Take several deep breaths and allow yourself to relax. When you feel centered, consider what you want to say and what you want out of the conversation.

Tip: If this is not the first time you have wanted to talk about a particular topic, think about the last time you did and see where you might not have been as assertive or empathic as you could have been.

2. Use "I" statements. Start your statements with "I." Remember that what you are talking about is how you feel and what you think. People can take "You" statements as accusations, which makes it more likely that there will be conflict in the conversation. (See also the <u>You vs. I</u> table.)

3. Use positive language. Using positive language can help you communicate your thoughts and feelings assertively but not aggressively. For example, instead of saying, *"I don't want to do that,"* say, *"I prefer to do something else."*

4. Set boundaries. Asserting your limits is essential in any relationship. Let your partner know what you are uncomfortable with, and be willing to say no when necessary.

For example, say your partner has a habit of canceling plans at the last minute, which makes you feel disappointed and unimportant. To assert your boundary, you could say, *"I understand that things come up, but when you cancel plans at the last minute, it makes me feel hurt and disrespected. In the future, can we agree to make plans that we're both committed to keeping?"*

In this example, you are honest with your partner about how their behavior affects you while showing empathy for their perspective by acknowledging that things can come up unexpectedly.

5. Compromise. Being an assertive communicator does not mean always getting your way. Seek compromise by finding common ground and working together to find a solution that works for both of you.

For example, say you and your partner have different ideas about how to spend your weekend. You want to take a relaxing day trip to the beach while your partner wants to hike. To seek compromise, you could say, *"I understand that you want to go hiking, but I prefer to go to the beach. What if we go on a shorter hike in the morning and then spend the afternoon at the beach?"*

When communicating with your partner, kindness and compassion are essential. Listening, responding, and speaking with empathy is the secret to building a deep connection between you in your relationship. Empathy has much to do with reading, sensing, and communicating emotions. And for that, it is best to develop one's emotional intelligence.

4

COMMUNICATING WITH EMOTIONAL INTELLIGENCE

"The more emotionally intelligent a couple — the better able they are to understand, honor, and respect each other and their marriage — the more likely they will live happily ever after."

— JOHN. M. GOTTMAN

E motional intelligence (a.k.a. emotional quotient or EQ) refers to your ability to recognize, understand, and manage your own emotions, as well as the emotions of others. People with high EQ can recognize their emotional states, effectively manage their responses, and respond to the emotions of others in a way that is empathetic and supportive.

Psychologists Peter Salovey and John D. Mayer developed the concept of emotional intelligence in the early 1990s. They defined emotional intelligence as "the ability to monitor one's own and others' feelings and emotions, to discriminate among them, and to use this information to guide one's thinking and actions." However, the term "emotional intelligence" gained widespread recognition and popularity through the work of author and journalist Daniel Goleman, who wrote the best-selling book *"Emotional Intelligence"* in 1995.[1]

One way to think about EQ is to imagine a situation where someone cuts you off in traffic. A person with high EQ might take a few deep breaths and then decide to let the incident go, recognizing that the other driver may be in a rush or have made a mistake. A person with low EQ might respond with anger and frustration, honking their horn and yelling out the window.

In short, a person with a high EQ can be mindful or self-aware and take a moment to look at the big picture and consider other people's perspectives. Their emotions do NOT control them. In contrast, a person with a low EQ cannot always take that mental step back and often reacts according to their emotions (not logic).

Emotional intelligence can make a big difference in building stable, long-term relationships.[2,3] Here are some reasons why developing your EQ contributes to your relationship.

Enhances Communication: EQ helps partners communicate effectively and understand each other's needs, emotions, and perspectives. High-EQ couples can better express their feelings without blaming or attacking each other, leading to more productive conversations and a deeper understanding of each other.

Builds Empathy and Connection: EQ fosters empathy in a relationship. As we discussed, this is required to create a deep connection between partners.

Promotes Understanding: EQ helps couples understand each other's emotional triggers, which can prevent misunderstandings and conflicts. When couples have a deeper understanding of each other, they are better equipped to navigate difficult situations and resolve disputes respectfully and productively.

Increases Resilience: EQ promotes resilience, which is important for weathering relationships' inevitable ups and downs. When you and your partner are emotionally intelligent, you will find that problems do not easily daunt you and arrive at solutions faster.

TOP 9 SIGNS YOU NEED TO DEVELOP YOUR EQ

Unfortunately, blaming in a relationship implies that you, and most likely your partner as well, need to improve your emotional intelligence. If you are unsure, the following are some common indicators of someone that needs to up their EQ. Do you recognize yourself in any of them?

1. **Lack of Self-Awareness**: You struggle to identify your own thoughts, emotions, and behavior. And since you are confused, you express them in unhealthy ways.
2. **Struggles With Empathy:** You find it difficult to understand or relate to your partner's or other people's emotions and perspectives. As such, it is hard for you to show compassion.
3. **Poor Communication Skills**: You struggle to communicate your emotions and thoughts effectively. You also have trouble listening to others, which leads to many misunderstandings.
4. **Trouble Managing Stress:** You find it difficult to cope with stress and let your emotions control you rather than the other way around.
5. **Difficulty Building and Maintaining Relationships:** You must work hard to connect with others on an emotional level. You find it difficult to "let others in" and struggle to form strong, positive relationships with others.

6. **A Tendency to React Impulsively:** You have a habit of reacting impulsively to situations without considering the emotional impact of your actions.

7. **An Inability to Take Constructive Feedback:** You have trouble accepting feedback and criticism. You see either as personal attacks, so you usually ignore them or get angry at the person who offered them. As a result, you cannot make positive changes based on their feedback.

8. **Difficulty Adapting to Change:** You struggle to adapt to change and new situations and find it hard to regulate your emotions when faced with uncertainty.

9. **A Tendency to Blame Others for Your Problems**: You blame others for your problems rather than taking responsibility for your thoughts, emotions, and actions.

Did you notice that self-awareness is at the top of the list above? You see, while you have influence, you do not have control over others. So, if you want to avoid blaming in your relationship, the first adjustment you should make is within yourself.

BUILDING YOUR SELF-AWARENESS

"The only person you can control is yourself. You alone have the power to choose: how you feel, your attitude, your behavior, your response."

— *MELISSA SPINO*

Self-awareness refers to the ability to recognize and understand your own thoughts, emotions, and behaviors. It involves being conscious of your existence as a unique individual with unique experiences and perspectives. In other words, self-awareness is the ability to reflect on yourself; it allows you to understand who you are, what you want, and why you do what you do.

How do you improve your self-awareness? Here are a few tips:

1. Practice mindfulness. Mindfulness is being fully present and aware of your thoughts, feelings, and bodily sensations in the moment. By practicing mindfulness regularly, you can become more aware of your thoughts and emotions and learn to observe them without judgment.

WORKSHEET: Mindfulness Breathing

Start practicing mindfulness with a simple **Mindfulness Breathing technique** in Appendix A.

2. Journal. Writing down your thoughts and feelings can help you identify patterns in your thinking and behavior and gain insight into your emotions. Here is a tip: whenever you feel unpleasant emotions and want to get angry or say mean things to your partner, grab your journal and a pen instead. Write down what you want to say. Let go, and do not censor yourself. Afterward, do something relaxing (e.g., walk in nature, take a hot bath, look at happy pictures of yourself and your partner, etc.). After some time, read what you wrote in your journal. Do you feel the same? What do you think of the *words* you used? What do you think of the *emotions* that poured out of you?

3. Ask for feedback. Ask trusted friends, family members, or coworkers what they think about how you speak and act. Listen to what they say with an open mind and the desire to learn and improve.

4. Take personality assessments. Take online personality assessments that can help you better understand your strengths, weaknesses, and tendencies.

5. Reflect on past experiences. Think about your past and how it has made you who you are today. Think about what you learned from it and how you can use that knowledge in the future.

6. Be open to new experiences. Trying new things can help you learn more about yourself and your preferences. Step outside your comfort zone and challenge yourself to try new activities or meet new people.

You may think that developing self-awareness is only for your benefit, but that is untrue. It does wonders for your relationship as well!

First, **self-awareness brings clarity to your relationship**. If you genuinely know what you need and can communicate it effectively to your partner, then there is no ambiguity in the relationship. When things are clear between you, misunderstandings and conflict will occur less often, lowering the chance of blaming each other when things go wrong.

Second, **self-awareness leads to better decision-making**. If you know and understand yourself better, you will make better choices. This, in turn, will make you a happier person. And a happy person in a relationship does wonders for the relationship itself.

Finally, **your self-awareness can rub off on your partner**. A self-aware person is likely to encourage the same behavior in others. Partners who support one another to be healthy, happy, and self-sufficient make for successful relationships.

PUTTING EQ INTO YOUR COMMUNICATIONS

A great relationship is defined by how well partners communicate with each other. After you build your self-awareness, it is time to ensure that you and your partner are communicating with emotional intelligence. Here are some tips on how to accomplish this.

1. **Actively listen and empathically reply.** When you disagree with your partner, do not respond immediately with your point of view. Instead, say, "I understand your disappointment, but you do realize that … ." Empathize with their feelings before sharing your thoughts. This way, your partner knows you are hearing them, not dismissing them.
2. **Avoid personal attacks.** During arguments, refrain from issuing personal attacks such as insulting your partner, using inappropriate or intimidating body language, etc. Personal reproaches do not solve anything; they only make arguments worse.
3. **Always speak calmly.** A highly charged discussion will worsen if you start shouting or yelling. High EQ partners always communicate with maturity and respect for each other.
4. **Seek explanations.** High EQ couples aim to understand each other's point of view even if they disagree. The goal is to understand your differences, not to focus on the actual difference. For example,

say you and your partner disagree about which school your child should attend. Instead of saying, "You are unbelievable!" or "Why can't you see this my way?" say, "I am trying to see your point of view here. Can you tell me why you are against this school?"

5. **Appreciate your partner.** No one has ever felt bad after receiving a compliment. Often, partners are so used to each other that they take each other for granted. High EQ couples understand the importance of appreciating each other in their relationship, even for the most minor things. For example, is your partner the one who is always taking out the garbage? If so, say, "Thanks for always taking the garbage out, babe."

6. **Aim for a relationship of equals.** High EQ couples acknowledge their influence on each other. However, they know that no one should try to control the other. No one is "the boss." So during communications, do not adopt an authoritative voice, put down, or ridicule your partner. Remember, they are your equals in your relationship.

COMMUNICATING YOUR BOUNDARIES

You set boundaries for yourself and others to establish healthy and appropriate relationships. These limits can be physical, emotional, mental, or even spiritual. They are meant to protect your well-being and promote respect and mutual understanding. Note that boundaries can be flexible and may vary depending on the situation and the people involved. Still, they are generally established to promote healthy interactions and prevent harmful behaviors or situations.

Often, blaming is present in a relationship due to a lack of boundaries. This can happen for various reasons, such as the following.

1. **Lack of Self-Awareness:** Suppose you are unaware of your needs, values, and limits. In that case, you may struggle to set clear and effective boundaries in your relationship. (**Tip**: See Building Your Self-Awareness.)

2. **Fear of Conflict:** You may avoid setting or enforcing boundaries out of fear of upsetting your partner or causing conflict. You may prioritize maintaining harmony over asserting your needs and desires.

3. **Codependency:** You may have a codependent relationship dynamic in which one relies heavily on the other for emotional, mental, physical, or financial support. If this is the case, you or your partner may find it hard to establish boundaries for fear of losing the help the other provides.

4. **Manipulation or Coercion**: In some cases, one partner may intentionally or unintentionally

manipulate or coerce the other partner into disregarding their boundaries.

5. **Cultural or Societal Norms:** In some cultures or societies, expectations or norms around romantic relationships may make setting and enforcing boundaries challenging. For example, there may be pressure to prioritize the relationship over individual needs or to conform to traditional gender roles.

Whatever the reason, the lack of boundaries can negatively affect your relationship. Over time, boundaries that continuously get crossed build resentment between you. It also breeds a lack of trust, loss of individuality, and even a lack of intimacy.

So, how do you create healthy boundaries with your partner?

1. It starts with YOU. Before discussing boundaries with your partner, take some time to identify your needs and limits first.

WORKSHEET: Identifying Your Boundaries

Not sure about your limits? Take the **Identifying Boundaries in Your Relationship** exercise in Appendix A.

---

2. Communicate clearly and assertively. Once you have identified your boundaries, communicate them clearly and assertively to your partner. Use "I" statements to express your feelings and needs.

3. Do not look back; look forward. Usually, talking about boundaries stems from a previous situation or event. However, as you communicate with your partner about your limits, refrain from looking back and focusing on what went wrong, which can instigate blaming.

Example: *"I feel confused and lonely when we cannot sit down and talk about our cultural differences in food and eating. Can we agree about not making fun of me when I use chopsticks during meals?"*

4. Respect your partner's boundaries. Boundaries are personal. You have lines you do not want to be crossed, as does your partner. So, do not force your partner to do as you wish. Give them the same courtesy if you are free to do your own thing.

For instance, say you want to honor your religion by attending church every Sunday morning. However, your partner is an atheist and does not want to go. In this regard, your boundary is communicating to your partner that you need Sunday mornings to attend church, not asking or telling your partner to go with you.

5. Reevaluate as needed. Boundaries can change over time, so it is crucial to reevaluate your boundaries periodically to ensure they reflect your needs and values while respecting your partner's.

Remember that setting boundaries in relationships is not about controlling or manipulating your partner but promoting mutual respect, understanding, and well-being. It is important to approach setting limits with empathy and a willingness to work together to create a healthy and fulfilling relationship.

Emotional intelligence plays a significant role in relationships. It improves communication, promotes understanding, builds strong connections, and strengthens your bond to withstand future challenges. EQ starts with you, so building your self-awareness is critical. Once you are more self-aware, identify your boundaries (needs and limits) and communicate them effectively with your partner.

When talking about boundaries, you are bound to talk about your emotions as well. And this is not as easy as most people think. In the next chapter, you will learn more about your feelings and how to express them to your partner.

5

HOW TO COMMUNICATE YOUR EMOTIONS

"Communication is the lifeline of any relationship. Without it, the relationship will starve itself to death."

— *ELIZABETH BOURGERET*

Talking about emotions is not easy. We are not really taught how to do this. In truth, most of us have learned to suppress what we think and feel to preserve harmony, evade embarrassment, avoid conflict, etc. But then, we reach a time when too much is too much, and we just explode, often in anger and accusations.

So the first step to communicating your emotions is to understand them. Why? Because you cannot effectively communicate what you do not understand.

UNDERSTANDING YOUR EMOTIONS

If you understand your emotions and the reason(s) behind them, you can express them more effectively to your partner. In turn, your partner will understand you better. Here are some tips to understand your feelings better.

All your emotions are valid. First, remember that all your emotions are valid. Sometimes you may think your feelings are bad, inappropriate, or wrong, so you should not feel or communicate them. However, emotions are reactions to internal or external stimuli. Your emotions are automatic responses to something. As such, they are always valid.

Label your emotions. According to psychologist Dr. Paul Ekman[1], humans have six primary emotions: happiness, sadness, fear, surprise, disgust, and anger. So, pick one or two from this list that apply to your feelings.

Dig deeper. Suppose you think your feelings are not any of the six primary emotions. In that case, you are probably feeling a secondary emotion.

Secondary emotions are reactions that arise in response to our primary emotions and are often more reflective of our thoughts and beliefs. For instance, you may find the words "annoyed," "numb," and "frustrated" more suitable for your feelings. However, if you think about it, these words lead to the primary emotion of anger.

Are you still confused about what you are feeling? Here is a quick table to help you based on psychologist Robert Plutchik's Wheel of Emotions or Feelings Wheel.[2]

What Emotion Are You Feeling?		
Primary Emotions	**Secondary Emotions**	
Happiness	Playful	Aroused
		Cheeky
	Content	Free
		Joyful
	Interested	Curious
		Inquisitive
	Proud	Successful
		Confident
	Accepted	Respected
		Valued
	Powerful	Courageous
		Creative
	Peaceful	Loving
		Thankful
	Trusting	Sensitive
		Intimate
	Optimistic	Hopeful
		Inspired

What Emotion Are You Feeling?		
Primary Emotions	**Secondary Emotions**	
Surprised	Startled	Shocked
		Dismayed
	Confused	Disillusioned
		Perplexed
	Amazed	Astonished
		Awe
	Excited	Eager
		Energetic
Fear	Scared	Helpless
		Frightened
	Anxious	Overwhelmed
		Worried
	Insecure	Inadequate
		Inferior
	Weak	Worthless
		Insignificant
	Rejected	Excluded
		Persecuted
	Threatened	Nervous
		Exposed

What Emotion Are You Feeling?		
Primary Emotions	**Secondary Emotions**	
Anger	Let down	Betrayed
		Resentful
	Humiliated	Disrespected
		Ridiculed
	Bitter	Indignant
		Violated
	Mad	Furious
		Jealous
	Aggressive	Provoked
		Hostile
	Frustrated	Infuriated
		Annoyed
	Distant	Withdrawn
		Numb
	Critical	Skeptical
		Dismissive
Disgust	Disapproving	Judgmental
		Embarrassed
	Disappointed	Appalled
		Revolted

What Emotion Are You Feeling?		
Primary Emotions	**Secondary Emotions**	
Disgust	Awful	Nauseated
		Detestable
	Repelled	Horrified
		Hesitant
Sadness	Lonely	Isolated
		Abandoned
	Vulnerable	Victimized
		Fragile
	Despair	Grief
		Powerless
	Guilty	Ashamed
		Remorseful
	Depressed	Inferior
		Empty
	Hurt	Embarrassed
		Disappointed

Discover the "why" of your emotions. Now that you have labeled your feelings and dug deeper to find more accurate words to describe them, it is time to understand WHY you feel this way. Ask yourself questions like, *"What led me to feel this way?"* and *"What happened just before I felt this way?"*

The objective is to identify the underlying reason for what you are feeling. Often, we want to blame others for our emotions, but what we should do is understand why we experience them.

Here is an example:

What are you feeling?

I am angry.

Can you explain further (use secondary emotions)?

I feel annoyed and let down.

What happened just before you felt angry?

My partner was late coming home.

WHY is this making you angry?

Because I asked them beforehand to be home early, and they said yes. So, I am annoyed.

WHY did you ask your partner to come home early?

I need them to help me prepare for our dinner party tomorrow.

WHAT was the effect of your partner not coming home early?

I had to do all the food prep all by myself. So, now I am tired and cranky.

So now you know your WHY. You are angry because you expected your partner to help you with something you communicated beforehand. You are angry because your partner did not fulfill a promise.

In a blaming relationship, your reaction to your anger might be to say, *"Why do you always leave everything up to me?!"* or *"Why do you make promises you don't keep?!"* However, such a reaction will most likely trigger your partner to react in anger. The best way to communicate with your partner is to express your feelings, not what they did.

For example, say, *"Babe, I feel let down and annoyed that you did not come home early as you said you would to help me with dinner preparations for tomorrow. Did something happen?"*

Notice that the above statement leaves room for your partner to air their side. If they have a valid reason for being late, try to be open-minded while asking for help. For example, say, *"Oh, okay, I understand now. I didn't finish all the stuff for tomorrow, though. Do you have time to help me then?"* Take note that the preceding statement is asking for help, not demanding it.

Of course, it is understandable that you are not okay that your partner said yes to coming home early and did not. If you want to address this part, say, *"About coming home later than we discussed, I understand you had your reasons, and I can respect that. But can we agree that you give me a quick call or message whenever you are late? This way, I'm not worried and understand what is happening before you come home."*

Now that you understand your emotions more, it is time to express them to your partner.

COMMUNICATING YOUR EMOTIONS

After understanding and identifying your emotions, **take some to reflect on your emotions and bring yourself to calmness**. Talking to your partner about your feelings is difficult when you are tense. (**Tip**: Do <u>Mindfulness Breathing</u> to calm yourself.)

As you reflect on your feelings, **consider whether sharing them with your partner is helpful** because not all thoughts need to be shared. For example, say that you are annoyed with your partner over something. But then, upon deeper reflection, you realize your irritation is because you are stressed about a deadline at work and slept poorly last night. In this situation, discussing your feelings with your partner may only lead to an argument neither of you needs. It is better to deal with these emotions yourself rather than take out your stress on your partner.

Next, **think about what you want to say**. Here is a tip: when you begin a sentence with the phrase "I feel," do your best to make the third word an emotion. If you do not, you are most likely not expressing your feelings but a point of view, judgment, or critique.

When you are ready to talk to your partner, remember that **timing is everything**. Do not just download your emotions all of a sudden. Your partner may feel like they are being ambushed, and you will not get the results you want. So, select a time and place that is good for you both.

As you convey your emotions to your partner, you may want to request specific changes. If you do, always **ask for changes respectfully, thoughtfully, and gently**. You may want to try a technique called the "sandwich method." This communication technique calls for sandwiching your request between two positive or supportive statements.

Example: *"Babe, I feel frustrated. First, I just want to say how much I appreciate you and everything you do for me. However, I've been feeling a little frustrated lately with how you have been communicating with me. I feel like you are not listening to me, and I feel disconnected from you. But I know we can work on this together. I trust that we can find ways to improve our communication and deepen our connection even more. What do you think?"*

It is not easy to talk about your emotions. But remember that a relationship is not just about you. It is also essential that your partner shares their feelings with you.

HELPING YOUR PARTNER COMMUNICATE THEIR EMOTIONS

Often, both partners are not equally comfortable expressing their feelings. If your partner has difficulty with this, here are some tips that may help.

Make talking about feelings normal. Make talking about your feelings a habit, not an event. Your emotions are valid and essential, but when you say, *"We need to talk,"* or *"I am not happy; we need to talk,"* your partner often thinks of a long, uncomfortable conversation they want to avoid.

Instead, start your statements with, *"Babe, I want to discuss something. Do you have a few minutes?"* This removes the threat or danger sign your partner may see in their head. This way, when you express your emotions, they will be in a more welcoming and helpful state of mind.

Additionally, to avoid making feelings talks weird, do them regularly. For example, say, *"I was so happy when Meg unexpectedly brought me that bouquet of flowers! What about you, babe? Anything that made you happy or put a smile on your face today?"*

Recognize emotional clues for help. If something tells you that your partner is sad or is going through something, do not wait for them to open up, ask them about it.

Example: *"Hey, I think something is bothering you, honey. Want to talk about it?"*

Give them the floor. Do not interrupt, provide an opinion, or pass judgment as your partner discusses their emotions with you. Remember that they already find it difficult to express their feelings, so do not interrupt their story. (What is the best way to respond to a partner sharing their feelings? See Empathic Listening and Empathic Speaking.)

Emotions are what make us human. They are at our core, so you must be in tune with yourself by fully understanding your emotions. Once you do and want to communicate them to your partner, it is best to be considerate. Remember that not all feelings must be expressed, but when you do, be courteous. Also, remember that the two of you are in a relationship. So, encourage your partner to be aware of their feelings and feel free to talk to you about them.

Now that you are more comfortable with your feelings and ready to have more meaningful talks with your partner, you might want to start addressing your conflicts. These are not easy conversations to have. So, read the next chapter before entering these discussions.

THE IMPORTANCE OF REFLECTION

"Problems should be like speed bumps. You slow down just to get over it, but you don't let it stop you from heading to your destination." [1]

— *SONYA PARKER*

Let's take a breather – a moment to reflect on how things are going.

When Greg and I embarked on the journey of fixing our relationship, despite the slow shifts we were gradually beginning to see, it was a lot of work, and we had to make an effort to stop and appreciate how far we'd come.

So if things feel like they're going slowly right now, take heart. You have years of old habits to break, and it's to be expected that it will take a little time for all the good new ones you're picking up to take hold. Reflection is key – taking the time to celebrate the small wins and recognize the hard work both of you are doing. No matter how dark things have seemed, you *can* get yourselves back on track, and you're already doing a lot of the work that will get you there.

Since Greg and I not only saved our marriage but took it to new levels, I've been passionate about helping other couples to do the same, and I'd like to take this moment to ask for your support.

By leaving a review of this book on Amazon, you'll show other people who are struggling with their relationships where they can find a glimmer of hope and all the guidance they need to get back on track.

Simply by letting new readers know how this book has helped you and what they'll find inside, you'll not only direct them toward the information that will help them; you'll show them that no matter how they feel right now, there is hope – and Greg and I are testament to that.

From the bottom of my heart, thank you for your support. My goal is to help as many people as possible to lighten their load.

Scan the QR code for a quick review!

6

BLAME-FREE CONFLICT
RESOLUTION

"In every relationship, disagreements are inevitable. But it's not the disagreements that determine the health of a relationship, it's how you resolve them."

— *STEVE MARABOLI*

When two different individuals come together, conflict is inevitable. After all, it is unrealistic to expect two people to agree on everything all the time. The secret is learning how to resolve conflict healthily rather than fearing or avoiding it or resorting to blaming.

WHAT IS CONFLICT?

Conflicts are more than disagreements. They happen when one or both people feel threatened, even if the threat is not real. In romantic relationships, the threat may be a perceived attack on one's identity. You may feel your partner (or the conflict) is questioning who you are.

For example, say you and your partner disagree on how money should be handled in your relationship. You prefer to prioritize savings because this is how you were raised. Your partner, on the other hand, likes to invest in various things which you believe to be too unstable. The threat here may be that your beliefs about money are ignored or even attacked. Another common source of conflict between partners is intimacy. One may want to have more sex than the other. In this case, the latter may feel that their boundaries are constantly threatened and crossed.

Conflicts usually indicate unfulfilled needs concerning control, recognition, affection, or respect. When we are confronted with conditions that appear to threaten these basic human needs, conflict arises, and it is normal for people to react immediately and strongly.

Conflicts do not just disappear. If not addressed, conflict gets worse. Because we see conflicts as threats to our well-being, they stay with us until we face them and figure out how to deal with them.

Note that how we respond to conflict is usually based on our own perceptions of the situation, not always on the facts. Our upbringing, culture, values, life experiences, and other factors influence our perceptions. And since your partner has their own set of these, it is easy to understand why relationship problems arise.

Conflicts trigger strong emotions in us. So, suppose you are uncomfortable with your feelings or cannot regulate them when stressed. In that case, addressing conflicts and developing win-win solutions can seem extremely difficult.

However, remember that **conflict has nothing to do with love**. Strong disagreements and tensions between people in a relationship do not necessarily mean their love is weak or nonexistent. Just because you have conflicts with your partner does not mean you do not deeply and genuinely love them. Love is a separate and distinct emotion from conflict and can coexist with disagreements and differences. This leads us to the next point.

Conflicts are a chance to learn and grow. When you can work out your conflicts, it builds trust. You can feel safe knowing your relationship can get through problems and fights.

HOW TO EFFECTIVELY COMMUNICATE DURING CONFLICT

So many factors influence who we are. Our cultural and family backgrounds, childhoods, personalities, life experiences, and various other factors all impact how we think, feel, and behave. As such, conflicts are bound to happen in a relationship.

However, to stay together, you must rise above your differences. You need to address your conflicts. Now, before you sit down to talk, consider the following suggestions. They will help you and your partner stay on course and reach a solution rather than blame each other.

1. Write down the issue, and stick to it. Take a piece of paper and write down what should be resolved. This will help you and your partner stick to the topic at hand. Often, so many things are added to an issue that, at some point, you and your partner have no idea what you are fighting about. By writing down one specific problem to solve before talking to each other, you can focus on it and successfully find a solution instead of getting distracted by other issues.

2. Be optimistic. Enter the conversation with the right mindset. If you think your relationship situation is hopeless, it is almost certain that it will turn out to be true. Suppose you have already decided that things are not going well and will not get better. In that case, everything your partner says will always seem like a sign that things are worsening.

3. Choose the best time and place to talk. Do not talk about important things with someone you know is not in the right mind to listen. Choose a moment when you are both comfortable, relaxed, well-rested, fed, and not busy with anything else. Choose a peaceful location with few distractions. For example, initiate the discussion after having a good meal or while cuddling on the sofa.

4. Actively listen and empathically speak to each other. If you want to be heard, be quiet first. When your partner is speaking, listen attentively and resist the urge to interrupt, defend or justify yourself, or blame your partner. The more your partner believes they have been heard, the more likely they will listen to what you say. Also, as you listen to your partner, pay attention to points that make sense or that you can empathize with. When it is your turn to speak, remember that you should always do so empathically. (See also Assertive + Empathic Speaking: Hear and See Me Too.)

5. If your partner interrupts or is not actively listening, do not raise your voice and try to speak over them. What is more powerful is to pause, maintain eye contact with your partner, and in a calm tone say, *"I would like to finish what I'm saying, please,"* or *"I believe it is my turn to share my point of view now."*

6. Address the fear/threat/unfulfilled need. One of the most powerful ways to address conflict is not to react to what is being said but to address the reason behind the words.

Example:

They Say: "For goodness' sake! Why don't you ever do as you say?!"

[READ: I feel like I cannot rely on you. This does not make me feel secure in our relationship.]

Your Reply: "Babe, yes, I forgot this one. I'm sorry about that. But there are plenty of other instances where I do as I say. You can rely on me."

They Say: "You never do anything around the house!"

[READ: I'm tired, and I need help. I feel like I don't have a life partner.]

Your Reply: "Babe, how can I help?"

7. **Make "repair attempts."** Happy couples are proficient at *repair attempts*, according to Dr. John Gottman, a recognized authority on the science of romantic relationships. Repair attempts are anything you do or say to keep a disagreement from spiraling out of control. They are like brakes that you apply to lower stress levels and prevent emotions from running away. It should be noted, however, that repair attempts are not intended to avoid discussing conflict. Their purpose is to give you and your partner a break until you both feel capable of communicating in a way that strengthens rather than ruins the relationship.

Here are some examples of repair attempts to say or do when things look like they are starting to escalate.

"I think we are at a point where we feel the need to prove our points, and no one wants to back down. Shall we take a short breather?"

"Can we take a few minutes to slow things down before they get out of control?"

"Wait, I'm not sure we are talking about the same thing. Can we backtrack a bit?"

"I'm not sure we are really hearing each other right now. What do you say we take a break and return to this later tonight?"

For some couples, touch or simple gestures work better than words. For example, you can touch your partner's hand as a gesture of support or indicate they need to slow down. For others, humor does the trick. See what works for you and your partner.

8. Focus on solutions. Instead of blaming and focusing on what is wrong, think of ways to make things right. For example, instead of shouting and making accusations about your partner not doing enough around the house, ask if it would help if you create a chore chart so that everyone knows who is doing what and when.

Important: In times of conflict, always look for win-win solutions. Remember that if the solution is not agreeable to both of you, everyone loses. If it does not look like a win-win answer is possible, find a way to compromise or take turns giving in.

9. Point out the benefits of finding solutions and moving forward. For example, say, *"I really do not enjoy getting upset and being a nag about household chores. So I think the chore chart will help us both. What do you think?"*

10. Limit the time you spend in confrontation. Do not go round and round in circles during a disagreement. Accept that you and your partner have reached a stalemate and take a breather. Why? Continuing to engage in an intense debate after a certain point is frustrating and potentially damaging —to the relationship and to you. Your limits are only known to you and your partner. And because you may have different thresholds, discuss this at another time when you are not in conflict.

11. If you decide to take a break, establish when you will reconnect. Alright, you have decided to take a break from discussing your conflict. Before stepping away from each other, determine when you will reconnect to discuss this topic again. For example, instead of continuing your discussion in the dining room, agree on a 20-minute break and meet in the living room. However, as a rule, do not take a break for more than 24 hours because it may do more harm than good. Resentment may develop between you, or one may want to avoid the discussion altogether.

Use the break for self-care. You guys took a break to calm yourselves down, so do that. For example, do a <u>Mindfulness Breathing</u> exercise, watch funny YouTube videos, listen to soothing music, etc. Do whatever you need to do to bring down your emotional level.

12. Reflect on yourself. After an argument, it is easy to pinpoint everything your partner did to contribute to the disagreement. This time, though, turn the focus on yourself. Ask yourself questions such as the following:

"Did I actively listen?"

"Did I understand their point of view?"

"Did I say or do something that made our argument worse?"

"Did I blame or accuse them of anything?"

"Did I criticize them?"

"Did I attack or shame my partner?"

"Am I regretting anything right now?"

The idea here is to understand your own conflict style and determine if there is anything you are saying or doing that is contributing to the dispute rather than solving it.

If you have determined you are indeed contributing to the conflict, ask yourself, *"What can I do better?"*

If you want, you can even discuss this with your partner. When you are both calm, bring up your argument and ask, *"Hey, did I say or do anything during our argument that you did not like at all? Was anything below the belt for you?"* If your partner pinpoints something, do not defend it. (Remember, you asked.) Just hear them out, ponder it, and see if you need to work on it.

As you and your partner discuss your conflict, one or both of you may need to hear two very important words: I'm sorry.

THE IMPORTANCE OF SAYING "I'M SORRY"

An apology is a statement of guilt or remorse for something you said or did that hurt your partner's feelings, made them feel bad, or caused harm or offense. Apologies are essential not just for your relationship but for yourself.

Why You Should Own Up to Your Mistakes

Apologies enable you to make better decisions. The inability to own up to your mistakes distorts your own reality. If you refuse to accept that something you said or did is inappropriate or wrong, you will keep doing the same thing. This reduces your ability to make sound decisions.

Saying sorry shows that you are taking responsibility for your actions and acknowledging their impact on your partner. It demonstrates that you care about your partner's feelings and are willing to try to repair any damage caused.

Owning up to your mistakes enables you to learn and grow. Simply put, you cannot learn from your mistakes if you do not recognize them. And if you do not learn from your mistakes, you will repeat them. That is just a prescription for getting nowhere in life.

Apologizing helps restore trust and connection in a relationship. When a partner feels hurt or betrayed, an apology can help to validate their feelings and create a sense of understanding and empathy. This can open a space for communication and healing, ultimately strengthening the relationship.

Saying sorry helps prevent future conflicts by acknowledging the mistake and committing to making positive changes. It sets a positive example for healthy communication and conflict resolution. It can also help to build a foundation of mutual respect and understanding in the relationship.

In contrast, the inability to own up to your mistakes endangers your partner's respect for you. You may hide your mistakes from your partner because you worry they will think less of you. However, they often already *know* you have made a mistake and are waiting for you to take responsibility. Unfortunately, for some people, saying *"I'm sorry"* is the hardest thing to do.

Why Apologizing Is Hard

Apologizing makes you feel "less than." For some people, saying sorry feels like admitting they are less than their partners and cannot do it because they think they need to be the boss in the relationship. For others, saying sorry translates to *"I am not good enough."* They are admitting that something is wrong with them instead of just committing a mistake.

Apologizing means you are guilty. Some people think that if they say sorry first after a fight, they admit guilt and, as such, are responsible for the whole argument, even if both sides did wrong. They think that if they apologize first, the other person will not have to take responsibility for their part in the fight.

However, many people want to hear *"I'm sorry"* just for hurting them. This has nothing to do with guilt. Saying sorry because your partner got hurt means you care about their feelings and do not like seeing them sad or in pain. This will help your partner feel safe with you and in your relationship.

Now, saying sorry may be difficult for the above reasons, but when it comes to relationships, this two-word phrase can do wonders for your relationship. If you are confused about when you should apologize to your partner, here are a few reasons to consider:

- when you hurt your partner's feelings or insult them
- when you act in a way that disrespects your partner or your relationship
- when you did something wrong, unfair, or hurtful, even though you knew it was wrong
- when you break a promise you made

Apologizing to someone you love can be challenging. Still, it is essential for repairing any damage caused and strengthening your relationship. Following are some tips on how to apologize effectively.

How to Apologize

1. Take responsibility. Start by acknowledging your role and taking responsibility for mistakes or hurtful actions. Do not make excuses or blame your partner or other people.

Example: *"I'm sorry I made fun of you in front of our friends. I realize that I embarrassed you. I'm sorry you felt that way."*

NOT: *"I'm sorry I made fun of you in front of our friends. You were smiling a bit, so I thought you were okay with it!"*

2. Express remorse. Let your partner know you feel sorry for what happened and its impact on them. Show empathy and try to understand their perspective.

Example: *"I'm sorry I made fun of you in front of our friends. I wish I could take it back."*

3. Be specific. Explain what you are apologizing for and be clear about what you will do differently in the future to prevent similar situations from occurring.

Example: *"I'm sorry I made fun of you in front of our friends. I will not do that again."*

4. Actively listen. Give your partner space to express their feelings and listen carefully to what they have to say. Avoid becoming defensive or dismissive of their concerns.

Example: *"I hear you, babe. I understand you felt embarrassed."*

NOT: *"It was just a joke!"*

5. Offer to make amends. Depending on the situation, you may need to offer to make amends or find a way to repair any damage caused. This could include doing something special for your partner or simply asking what you can do to make them feel better.

Example: *"I'm sorry I made fun of you in front of our friends. I wish I could take it back. How can I make this up to you?"*

6. Follow through. Once you have apologized, follow through on any commitments or promises, demonstrating your sincerity and commitment to positive changes in your relationship.

Important: Do not expect automatic forgiveness. Saying you are sorry does not mean your partner must forgive you or immediately be okay with what you have said or done.

Remember that apologizing is just the first step in repairing any damage caused. It takes time, effort, and commitment to rebuild trust and connection in a relationship. By taking responsibility for your actions and showing your partner that you care, you can start the process of healing and strengthening your relationship.

Why Accepting an Apology Is Hard

It is not always easy to forgive. People might not want to forgive and forget for many reasons, even after an apology. Following are some of these reasons:

The apology does not feel genuine. If your partner's apology feels insincere or forced, it can be difficult to accept it. You may feel like they are just saying what you want to hear rather than taking responsibility for their actions.

What to Do: Let them know what you need to feel like they are taking responsibility for their actions. You could also ask them to explain why they are sorry and what they plan to do differently in the future.

The hurt is still raw. Depending on the situation, it may take time for you to process your emotions and feel ready to accept an apology. It can be hard to let go of those feelings and move forward if you are still feeling hurt or angry.

What to Do: Communicate with your partner about what you are going through and let them know you need time to heal before you can fully move on. You could also consider seeking support from a respected friend, family member, therapist, or counselor to help you process your emotions.

You do not trust your partner. Suppose your partner has repeatedly let you down or broken promises in the past. In that case, believing their apology is genuine can be challenging. You may feel like they will just hurt you again, making it difficult to accept their apology.

What to Do: Rebuilding trust takes time and effort, but it is possible. Discuss your concerns with your partner and explore ways to rebuild trust together. This could include setting boundaries, being transparent and honest with each other, and following through on commitments.

You have a hard time letting go of grudges. Some people find it difficult to let go of past hurts and may hold onto grudges even after an apology. If this sounds like you, exploring why you hold onto those feelings may be helpful.

What to Do: If you find it difficult to let go of past hurts, it may be helpful to work on forgiveness and letting go with the help of a close friend, family member, or even a therapist or counselor. You could also try practicing mindfulness or meditation to help you let go of negative thoughts and emotions.

You are just not ready to forgive. Accepting an apology is often a step toward forgiveness, but that does not mean you are obligated to forgive immediately. It is okay to process your feelings and decide when to forgive your partner.

What to Do: Communicate with your partner about where you are and what you need to work toward forgiveness. (See also Worksheet: How to Forgive.)

TOP 14 WORDS AND PHRASES TO AVOID WHEN COMMUNICATING WITH YOUR PARTNER

Communication is vital in any relationship. So far, we have discussed what to say and how to say it. But what about the words you should not say or at least avoid saying when communicating with your partner?

Keep in mind that you want to stay away from blaming each other. Consider how these simple words and phrases might trigger blaming as you read the list below.

1. Actually

Using the word "actually" can sometimes come across as aggressive or correcting your partner's perspective, making them feel defensive or invalidated. Of course, everyone makes mistakes. But the next time you catch your partner making one, avoid correcting them with an "actually" because it may appear as if you are sticking it in their face or rectifying them.

Example: *"Actually, you're wrong about that."*

Better: *"I think I see things differently. Can you explain why you see it that way?"*

2. But

The word "but" is probably one of English's most used and abused words. It is used to casually dismiss or ignore someone's remarks. What they say does not matter because you have a better idea. And mind you; your partner picks up on this. To them, a "but" means you did not hear them.

Example: *"What you said about dinner is good, but maybe we should order in instead."*

Better: *"I'm not really in the mood for Chinese food. Are you ok with pizza or something else?"*

3. Assume

Using the word "assume" (or any of its forms) can be problematic because it often implies that you are making judgments or drawing conclusions without all the information. It may also suggest that you are not paying attention to your partner.

Example: *"I assumed you are okay with friends dropping by for dinner this weekend."*

Better: *"Greg and Amanda want to drop by for dinner this weekend. Are you feeling up to that?"*

4. The F Word

Some people are okay with the "F" word, while others find it offensive, immature, and impolite. So, using this word is up to you and your partner. However, I would advise refraining from using this word whenever trying to resolve conflict.

5. Honestly

Have you ever noticed how the word "honestly" is said before someone says something dishonest? Consider this: if you genuinely believe what you are saying, what difference does the word "honestly" make? None. So, just avoid it and say whatever you need without relying on it. Be sure what you want to say, or wait until you are more certain before saying it. Also, "honestly" in relationships can easily be construed as insincere or dismissive.

Example: *"Honestly, I don't care what we have for dinner."*

Better: *"I'm open to what you want for dinner. What are you in the mood for?"*

6. No Offense

Like "honestly," most people say "no offense" when they are about to offend someone. Worse, they *know* they will offend someone and try to soften the blow by saying this phrase first. "No offense" is a defense mechanism used by people who want to be nasty but do not want to be obvious about it.

Example: *"No offense, but you should take a shower or something."*

Better: *"Honey, I don't want to hurt your feelings, but I noticed you might feel a bit sweaty or dirty. How about we shower together or separately to feel fresh and comfortable?"*

7. Personally

Using the word "personally" can sometimes be dismissive or self-centered, implying that your opinion or experience is better or the only one that matters. The term is also avoidant in nature. For instance, if your partner says, *"We are invited to Mark's 50th birthday two weekends from now. Do we have anything planned?"* And you reply, *"Personally, I do not think we should go to that party."* Note that you are not saying *"yes"* or *"no"* or providing any explanation. Just skip "personally" and start with the word that usually comes after it—"I."

8. Try

Using the word "try" can sometimes come across as non-committal or lacking in confidence, implying that you may not be fully committed to a course of action. Of course, no one should make promises they cannot keep. However, "try" is a weak form of any attempt.

Example: *"I'll try to attend your event next week."*

Better: *"I'll do my best to attend your event next week. Give me the details so I can check my work calendar and let you know immediately."*

9. Whatever

Using "whatever" can come across as dismissive or uninterested in your partner's feelings or perspective.

Example: *"Whatever, I don't care."*

Better: *"I'm not sure how I feel about that. Can you explain further? I want to understand your view."*

10. That's Not My Problem

Using the phrase "that's not my problem" can dismiss your partner's feelings or concerns, damaging the trust and closeness in your relationship. For example, if your spouse comes to you with an issue, and you respond with *"That's not my problem,"* this can make them feel like their problem is not important to you and that you do not care about them. Instead, say, *"I'm sorry you're going through this. What can I do to help?"*

11. You're Overreacting/Calm Down

Using the phrase "You're overreacting" or "Calm down" can be dismissive of your partner's feelings and quickly escalate the conflict. Also, notice that using these phrases almost always has the opposite effect.

For example, say your partner is airing their side during a disagreement, and you respond with, *"You're overreacting."* This can make them feel that you are not listening or do not want to listen to their point of view. Additionally, they may think that their opinions are not valid or important to you, leading to further conflict.

A better approach would be to listen to their concerns and validate their feelings. You could say, *"I understand that this is upsetting for you. Can you tell me more about how you're feeling?"*

12. It's Not a Big Deal/Just Forget About It

Saying *"It's not a big deal"* or *"Just forget about it"* downplays your partner's feelings or concerns. It can make them feel like their emotions are not valid or important.

Example: *"Why are you angry? It's not a big deal."*

Better: *"I can see that you're angry. Can you tell me what's upsetting you?"*

Example: *"Geez, are you still upset about the game you missed? Just forget about it!"*

Better: *"I see you're still bummed out about missing the game. Tell me, what will make you feel better?"*

13. That's Just the Way I Am

Saying this phrase can show disregard for your partner's feelings or concerns, making them feel like you are unwilling to work on improving your behavior. For example, say your partner brings up an issue with something you said or did, and you respond with, *"That's just the way I am."* Such a response can make them feel like you are disregarding their feelings and opinions and are unwilling to change or try to address their concerns, leading to feelings of frustration and resentment.

A better approach would be to listen to their concerns and take ownership of your actions. You could say, *"I understand why that hurt your feelings, and I want to work on changing that behavior so it doesn't happen again."*

14. You Always/Never

Sentences starting with "You always" or "You never" are common in relationships where blame exists. This is probably one of the most damaging phrases you can say to each other because it is accusatory, judgmental, and definitive. Such a phrase can make the other person feel attacked and defensive.

Example: *"You never clean up after yourself!"*

Better: *"I feel frustrated when I see dirty dishes left in the sink. Can we work on cleaning up after ourselves more consistently?"*

To have a blame-free and solution-focused discussion about your conflict, it is crucial to know how to communicate effectively with your partner during times of dispute. Next, as you sit down to address your conflict, you must focus on the topic, remain calm, and strive to listen to each other rather than start going against each other.

Remember, the point of the discussion is to understand each other's different points of view and to arrive at a win-win solution. For this, saying two important words—*"I'm sorry"*—may be the most important thing you can do. Equally important is knowing what not to say when addressing conflict with your partner.

As you and your partner discuss your conflict, you may face another common relationship challenge—patience. The next chapter will help you with this.

7

THE POWER OF PATIENCE

"Patience is not simply the ability to wait. It's how we behave while we're waiting."

— *JOYCE MEYER*

I mpatience is a feeling of frustration or irritability that happens when we have to wait or when things do not happen the way we want them, as quickly as we want them. It can make you feel like time is moving too slowly, and you might get upset and irritated with yourself or others because you want things to happen faster.

WORKSHEET: Am I Impatient?

Are you mostly calm and relaxed or anxious and impatient? If you are unsure, take the quick **Am I Impatient Self-assessment Quiz** in Appendix A.

IMPATIENCE AND YOUR BRAIN

When we are impatient, we are not just unwilling to wait. Major frustration sets in almost immediately, and when this happens, it indicates that we are starting to turn off our prefrontal cortex, the part of your brain responsible for higher-level thinking.[1]

At the same time, we are engaging our *amygdala*, which is an almond-shaped fragment located in the middle of our brains. It forms part of the limbic system, a group of brain structures that help control our emotions (how we feel) and behavior (how we act).[2]

When the amygdala is activated like this, our thoughts and actions start veering away from logic. Stress and anger rise, and we now feel an intense emotional urge to lash out. Additionally, when we experience extreme emotions, our bodies send extra impulses to the brain, heightening the experience and warping our perception of time. As a result, 1 minute of waiting under extreme frustration can feel like 5 minutes!

Another component in how we perceive time is *control*. When we believe we have no control over something, such as the elevator's speed, when our partner decides to clean the garage, another driver's road behavior, etc., time appears to move more slowly.

When impatience reaches a higher degree of frustration and stress, we are more prone to lose self-control, empathy, and understanding. Thus, it is unsurprising that blame exists if one or both people in a relationship are impatient.

IMPATIENCE AND BLAMING

When you are impatient, you are likelier to lash out or blame your partner rather than take the time to understand their perspective during conflicts.

A lack of patience can also be linked to a desire for control, which may contribute to blaming behavior. For example, you may feel a sense of urgency to solve a problem during stressful situations. And if your partner appears to be progressing at a slower speed, you may wish to "take over" the issue entirely instead of letting them be.

Impatience may also lead you to look down on your partner. If you lack patience, you might get angry or upset with your partner if they do not meet your expectations or move at your desired pace. This can make you feel like you are better than your partner, and you might start to think they are not as competent or skilled as you are. Obviously, this can hurt your relationship because it can create a power imbalance and erode your trust and respect for each other.

REASONS FOR IMPATIENCE

There are various reasons why someone might be an impatient person. Here are a few potential factors:

1. **Personality Traits:** Some people may have personality traits predisposing them to impatience, such as being highly driven or goal-oriented. These traits can make it difficult to tolerate delays or setbacks.
2. **Environmental Factors:** Impatience can be exacerbated by environmental factors such as a fast-paced career or living in a congested city. It might be tough to slow down and be patient in a workplace where there is a lot of pressure to be productive or move swiftly.
3. **Mental Health Conditions:** Some mental health conditions, such as anxiety or attention-deficit/hyperactivity disorder (ADHD), can contribute to impatience. These conditions can make it difficult to focus or tolerate delays or distractions.

4. **Life Experiences:** Negative or stressful experiences, such as trauma or chronic stress, can contribute to impatience. These experiences can heighten a person's sense of urgency and make it difficult to be patient with themselves or others.

5. **Learned Behavior:** Impatience can also be learned through experiences with family, friends, or other influential people in a person's life. Suppose a person has grown up around impatient people or learned that impatience is the only way to get what they want. In that case, they may struggle to develop patience as an adult. (And speaking of *learned behavior*, today's modern world has also greatly contributed to developing our impatience.)[3,4]

6. **Instant Gratification**: With the rise of technology, we have become accustomed to getting what we want immediately. We can order goods online and have them delivered the same day or stream movies and TV shows instantly. This ability has created an expectation that things should always be available immediately, leading to impatience when waiting.

7. **Information Overload:** The internet has given us access to an overwhelming amount of information. We can quickly search for answers to any question, which means we are constantly bombarded with new information. This can make it harder to focus and lead to impatience when we have to sift through much information to find what we need.

8. **Busy Lifestyles:** Modern life is often fast-paced and demanding, with many people feeling like they don't have enough time to get everything done. This perceived time crunch creates a constant sense of urgency and impatience throughout the day.

9. **Social Media:** Social media platforms are designed to keep us engaged and scrolling through content—fast. This can make us feel like we must constantly check our phones, leading to impatience when we wait for notifications or updates.

So, we are not used to waiting in today's world. We want it all, and we want it NOW. However, this is not a normal expectation in yourself or any relationship.

BENEFITS OF WORKING ON YOUR PATIENCE

You may be living in an impatient world, but cultivating patience is perhaps one of the best things you can do for yourself. Here are some of the reasons why:

Less Stress: Impatience can cause stress and anxiety[5], but being more patient can help you feel calmer and more relaxed—more patience = more zen.

Improved Decision-Making: When you are impatient, you can make impulsive decisions without fully considering the consequences. By cultivating patience, you learn to take the time, consider your options, and make better choices.

Increased Focus: Impatience can make it hard to focus on a task because you constantly think about what you want to happen next. By developing more patience, you can stay present and focused on the present moment.

Improved Well-Being: Cultivating patience can help you feel more content and satisfied with your life as you learn to appreciate the present moment and take things one step at a time.

Better Relationships: Impatience can lead to conflicts and misunderstandings in relationships. By developing more patience, you may be able to communicate more effectively and avoid unnecessary arguments.

Freedom From Emotional Suffering: Impatience can create emotional suffering. Remember, *you* are the one feeling impatient; *you* are the one getting frustrated; *you* are the one getting angry; *you* are the one sighing, gritting your teeth, and so on. True, your impatience can negatively affect your partner too. Still, you are the first to suffer the burden of your impatience. Would you not rather be free of it?

So, as you can see, cultivating patience is beneficial not only to your relationship but also to your overall well-being!

HOW TO MAINTAIN YOUR PATIENCE DURING CONFLICT

As we have discussed, conflicts are a normal part of any relationship. To prevent their escalation, having patience is critical. Patience does not imply ignoring, overlooking, denying, or tolerating shortcomings. You always have the right to voice your concerns. Patience is healthily communicating these concerns, minus the anger, blame, and negativity.

So, how do you stay mindful and maintain your calm during conflicts? Here's how:

1. Start conflict discussion with an open mind. Shift your mindset from "fighting each other" to "hearing each other." Stop thinking, *How can I make them do what I want*, and shift to *What and why do they have a different view on this?* Couples frequently view conflict resolution as an opportunity to persuade, manipulate, or bully others into doing what they want, i.e., "my way." If this is your thinking, you have already put yourself in impatient mode.

Keep this word in mind: **"willingness."** You must be willing to hear your partner out. You must be ready to understand their point of view entirely. You must be willing to let go of "my way" if it is not a solution that works for both of you.

2. Actively listen to your partner and try to understand *their* perspective. Remember that it should be YOU+ME vs. CONFLICT, not YOU vs. ME. One of the ways to ensure that you are actively listening is to be able to answer this question: what is <u>their</u> viewpoint?

Imagine that someone will ask you later about your partner's perspective, and you should be able to answer them easily. If you cannot correctly relay it, then chances are you were not listening. (**Tip:** See also <u>Worksheet: Active Listening</u>.)

3. When it is your turn to speak, take a few deep breaths to center yourself before responding. If the discussion is heated, take a few deep breaths and count to ten before replying to your partner. Additionally, remember to always stay calm and avoid becoming defensive or argumentative.

Example: *"I hear/understand you. My point of view on this is ..."*

NOT: *"Why are you being difficult?!"*

4. Communicate clearly and respectfully, using "I" statements. Speak only for yourself!

Example: *"I don't think I'm explaining myself clearly."*

NOT: *"You're not hearing me!"*

Example: *"I don't feel like you prioritize me."*

NOT: *"You always put me second."*

Example: *"I feel down."*

NOT: *"You bring me down."*

5. Be careful with your non-verbal cues. Exhibit complete patience. Ensure you align your words with your posture, facial expression, hand gestures, etc. For example, do not keep one eye on the clock, sigh, tap your fingers, interrupt, clench your fists, etc.

6. Do not rush the process. Remember, you are equals in your relationship, and both of you should be able to express yourselves. So, do not jump to conclusions, make assumptions about your partner, offer simplistic answers, or short-cut the conversation by saying something like, *"This is what we should do."*

7. Watch out for your stress points. You know yourself best. What irritates you during discussions? What causes your impatience? Check all that apply:

☐ My partner is interrupting me.
Possible solution:
Say, *"Babe, I want to finish what I am saying."*

☐ My partner is raising their voice.
Possible solution:
Say, *"Can we not raise our voices? I feel agitated when you do that."*

☐ Someone is calling/texting me repeatedly.
Possible solution:
Put your phone on silent before your conversation, and ask

your partner to do the same.

☐ Others (list down any other impatience triggers and possible solutions)

_____

_____

_____

_____

_____

Reflect on your potential impatience triggers and plan how to handle them if and when they occur.

8. Take breaks or apply <u>repair attempts</u> as needed to avoid becoming overwhelmed or frustrated. Prevent emotions from escalating by stepping away from the conversation when needed. This will help you both regain energy and look at the situation differently.

9. Be flexible and learn the art of compromise. At the start of the conversation, especially if this is the first time you discuss the subject, remember that you do NOT have the whole picture. As you talk, new information may come to light. In this scenario, discuss the areas where you agree rather than focusing on the issues where you disagree.

For example, suppose that your partner always comes home late despite previous discussions that you do not like this. However, after a proper sit-down, your partner reveals that massive layoffs are happening at work. They feel they should show they are a team player willing to work long hours if necessary. In this instance, you may modify your attitude toward your partner's late arrival (at least for now), or you both make sacrifices. For example, if Thursday nights are the busiest for you, discuss the likelihood of your partner arriving home on time on these days.

Keep the above tips in mind during conflict resolution conversations. Additionally, please note the following.

Nip it in the bud. Sometimes conflict starts as a tiny problem you allow to grow into a major battle in your relationship. So, impatience occurs because of all that built-up frustration. For example, my friend Denise[6] once told me that she had a major fight with her partner Ian* about ... mixing socks and underwear in the wash.

The issue may sound trivial, but Denise has mild obsessive-compulsive disorder (OCD). However, since she was coping well with her condition, she decided she would not make this a big deal. She never addressed it with her partner. She let her tiny annoyance grow inside her day by day. After a year of living together, she started to see nearly everything as annoying about Ian. After one extremely difficult day, she came home, saw their disorganized living room and the mixed clothes in the hamper, and lost it. Tears, shouts, and hurtful words ensued. All this time, Ian was just bewildered. Later, they had a discussion, and it wasn't even difficult to ask Ian to start using different wash nets for his clothes. She said, *"All this time, I held back because I didn't want any conflict. I didn't realize I was slowly creating one."*

Impatience does not solve anything. Being impatient and losing your cool can either end or worsen the conversation. Either way, nothing gets solved.

Disagreement ≠ disrespect. Impatience can easily lead to disrespect. However, blaming, shouting, angry words and gestures, etc., have no place in conflict resolution. Just because you disagree about something does not mean that you cannot respect or value each other's opinions. Just because impatience creeps in does not allow you to disrespect another human being.

Here is a tip: imagine an emotional mirror. When you feel impatience, imagine your partner starting to feel the same. When you want to start gritting your teeth and staring down at your partner, imagine how it would feel if they were doing the same. If you feel like shouting and saying mean and hurtful words, internally say them to yourself first and see how you feel. In short, do not say or do anything you do not want to do to yourself.

Do you want to be right, or do you want to have peace? Alright, you have discussed your conflict at length but cannot agree on a win-win situation. Your patience is running thin now. So what do you do next? It is time to dig deep and consider if getting your way is the right way right now.

For instance, say you are struggling with weight and body image issues and want to change your lifestyle. However, your partner refuses to have anything to do with it and keeps bringing unhealthy comfort foods home (e.g., bags of chips, high-calorie soda, donuts, etc.) and eating them in front of you. You express that seeing them consume these food items in front of you damages what you want to achieve. Your partner believes you should not regulate their eating habits since they do not have any weight concerns. In this case, the conflict itself may add unnecessary stress to the lifestyle changes you want. If so, perhaps it is better to let the argument go, let your partner be, and keep the peace in your relationship.

Important: This does NOT mean you give in and change your plans! Opting for peace does not mean giving up doing what you want. You are just deciding that you and your partner will do different things on this specific matter. This also does not mean the discussion is done and dusted. Giving in now does not mean giving in forever. (Regarding the example above, studies show that a shift in one partner's health habits is frequently accompanied by a change in the other partner's behavior eventually. So, this particular conflict is definitely open to further discussion later.[7])

HOW TO DEAL WITH AN IMPATIENT PARTNER

What if you are cool-headed, calm, and patient, but your partner is not? Here are some tips for dealing with this situation.

1. Actively listen. (Yes, this one again.) Impatient people want to be heard. The minute they sense any inattentiveness, it is highly likely that their impatience will be triggered. So, hear them out, ask them their "why," validate what they said by reiterating their point of view, etc.

2. Do not meet any impatient outbursts. Listen to your loved one but know that engaging may not be necessary. Often, impatient people just want to vent. So, let them. If your partner's impatience is turning you off, leave the room. If you know that will worsen the situation, say, *"I can see you are sad/mad/annoyed/frustrated about something. I'll give you some room."*

Also, do not correct them during their outburst. Remember, saying things like, "Calm down," "You are overreacting," and "Get a grip" will only serve to feed the fire.

3. Set boundaries. If your partner's impatience is causing you stress or anxiety, it may be helpful to set boundaries. Let your loved one know what you need from them, and be clear about unacceptable behaviors.

Situation: Your partner likes to break dishes when impatient and angry.

Say: *"I understand something is bothering you. I just feel so stressed when you break dishes. I feel that the whole house is thrown into chaos when you do that. Can we agree on other ways for you to vent? How can I help here?"*

Situation: Your partner likes to smoke when impatient, and you are a firm non-smoker.

Say: *"Babe, you know my father died of throat cancer, so I don't support smoking. This is very important to me. Do you feel you can find other ways of coping? What do you think?"*

4. Be a force of positive influence. If your partner is impatient, remember that it took years to be that way, and they cannot just flip a switch and change. However, remember that as the other half of the relationship, you influence them. So, when the time is right, see if you can encourage them to be more patient.

For example, suppose your partner gets super irritated during traffic. They become impatient and note negative things around them (e.g., the car is dirty, why road construction must occur now, the other car's music is too loud, etc.). In this scenario, say something to distract them, like, *"Oh, how about we cook your favorite dinner tonight?"* or *"Are you in the mood for ice cream later?"* My yoga buddy, Abby[8], is more pointed by saying, *"Babe, quick! Say something positive or something you are grateful for right now."* It hinted to her husband that he was too impatient and negative for her liking.

5. Practice "radical acceptance." Radical acceptance is a concept in psychotherapy, specifically Dialectical Behavior Therapy[9]. It is the ability to accept something for what it is *without* trying to judge, change, or control the situation. It is complete acceptance; no ifs or buts.

We all want to be with someone who accepts us for who we are—flaws and all. We do not want to be changed, especially if it is for the sole convenience of the other person. So, suppose after exercising patience and positive influence, your partner is still impatient. You then need to remind yourself of all their positive qualities and ask yourself if their impatience is something you can live with.

6. Practice self-care! Dealing with an impatient partner can be draining. Take care of yourself by practicing self-care activities like exercise, meditation, getting enough sleep, or spending time with friends.

By now, you have learned many things about yourself, how to see things from your partner's perspective, communicate better, and effectively address conflict, but we are not done yet! In the following chapter, you will learn how to restore the trust and safety that blaming has undermined in your relationship.

8

REBUILDING TRUST AND SAFETY IN YOUR RELATIONSHIP

"Rebuilding a relationship is like building a house. You need a solid foundation and a good plan."

— *ANONYMOUS*

You need to be able to trust your partner and feel safe in the relationship you created. Unfortunately, conflicts, fighting, and blaming create a toxic environment that erodes these relationship foundations. To rebuild trust and safety, you must first acknowledge and accept responsibility for your behavior (as we have done in previous chapters). Next, you and your partner must be willing to move forward with a better relationship. How do you do that? Let us count the ways.

TOP 12 TIPS TO REBUILD TRUST AND SAFETY

1. **Take responsibility**. It cannot be stressed enough how important it is to own up to your mistakes and take responsibility for your actions in the past. If, at this point, you feel that you have committed zero mistakes, I encourage you to go over the previous chapters again. Remember, there are two of you in this relationship. It is almost impossible that its deterioration is the sole responsibility of one partner. Moving forward, be mindful of your thoughts, emotions, and behavior in your relationship.

2. **Apologize**. Sincerely apologize for any hurt or harm you may have caused and acknowledge the impact of your behavior on your partner. If you see that your partner is struggling with your apology or extending forgiveness, ask them what you can do to show them that you are sincere.

3. **Practice forgiveness**. Forgiveness is an integral part of rebuilding trust. If your partner apologizes, do your best to forgive. If you are not ready, tell them you need time or what you need from them. Additionally, be willing to forgive yourself for any wrongdoing that you may have done that

contributed to the erosion of your relationship. Also, practice true forgiveness. That is, when issues arise in the future, as they will most certainly do, do not bring up the past.

4. **Be patient**. Rebuilding trust takes time, so be patient and understand that you and your partner may need time to heal and feel safe again.

5. **Create and respect healthy boundaries**. As you move forward, you may realize that certain boundaries must be established to prevent previous problems. For example, you may have both gotten into the habit of raising your voices during arguments. Looking back, you realize how shouting made everything worse. So, "no shouting or raised voices during disagreements" may be a new healthy boundary for your relationship.

6. **Be consistent.** Consistency in your words and actions is essential for rebuilding trust. Show trustworthiness by following through on commitments and promises.

7. **Communicate openly**. Open communication is key to rebuilding trust. Share your thoughts, feelings, and concerns with your partner and encourage them to do the same. Remember to ask your partner open-ended questions. This makes them feel that you are genuinely interested in their thoughts and opinions, which increases emotional closeness.

8. **Be truthful.** Many couples trying to rebuild their relationships tend to sugarcoat certain things or only want to discuss positive or pleasant topics to not "rock the boat." Yes, your relationship may be a bit fragile right now, but if you want TRUST and SAFETY to return, you and your loved one must present your authentic selves in your relationship.

9. **Support each other.** Go back to the fundamental reason for starting a relationship: to experience this life together while supporting each other. So, ask each other about your dreams and goals. Life is not static, so you might be surprised to learn that your dreams and goals have shifted or their placement on your priority lists has changed. Whatever your individual or family goals are, support each other!

10. **COMMIT TO NO MORE BLAMING.** Do not undo all your hard work by reverting to blaming. When your emotions and impatience arise, address yourself first. For example, meditate, do mindful breathing exercises, watch funny YouTube videos, take a walk, make a gratitude list, etc.

11. **Stay positive.** Always focus on the positive aspects of your relationship as you rebuild trust and safety. Remember, you chose to stay together for a reason, so keep those reasons in mind.

12. **Seek support.** Your relationship depends on you and your partner. Sometimes, however, outside help may be necessary to ensure you are going in the

right direction. Speak with a trustworthy family member, another couple you respect and trust, or your pastor; consider seeing a therapist or counselor together.

WHAT TRUST IS NOT

You may not realize this, but there are a lot of misconceptions about trust in a relationship. Go over the list below and discuss them with your partner to ensure that you are on the same page and prevent future misunderstandings.

In a healthy relationship, trust is not:

1. Blind Faith: Trust is not about blindly believing everything your partner says or does without question. You each have a right to ask for clarifications.

2. 100% Access: Trust is not about controlling or monitoring your partner's every move or decision. For example, trust does not necessarily mean surrendering your social media accounts and passwords, having tracker software installed on your phone, providing the security code to your mobile phone, etc.

Important: Couples have different ways of showing trust. Many are okay with sharing these things and even have joint bank accounts. It is up to you and your partner to decide what information to share and what not to share.

3. Perfect: Trust is not about expecting yourself or your partner to be perfect or never make mistakes. Remember, we are all human.

4. Conditional: Trust is not about setting conditions or demands on your partner for them to earn your trust.

5. Willful Ignorance: Trust is not about ignoring red flags or warning signs indicating your partner may be untrustworthy. Nip doubts in the bud by immediately communicating your feelings and thoughts with your partner.

6. Keeping Score: If trust is keeping score, your mindset is set on creating a winner and a loser. This mentality is not set up for trust but for waiting for someone to make a mistake. Yes, do not ignore red flags. But when a red flag appears, address it and move on. Do not record it on a mental scorecard.

7. Static: Trust is not stationary; it requires ongoing effort and maintenance to keep it strong.

8. One-Sided: Trust cannot be built by just one partner; it requires effort and commitment from both of you. Also, trust should not be ME-focused. In a relationship, the more you focus on yourself and what you need, want, and desire, the less room there is for you to give your partner what they need, want, and desire. If you are both ME-focused, no one is fulfilled. So, stay away from the "what YOU need to do to rebuild trust" mentality and move to "what WE need to do to feel we can trust each other."

RELATIONSHIP CHECK-INS

Relationship check-ins are another way to rebuild trust and safety in your relationship. These are scheduled talks that allow you to check on the condition of your relationship, discuss any difficulties or concerns, and ensure that both of you are on the same page.

Following are some examples of relationship check-ins. You do not have to do all of these. Just decide which one(s) would be most beneficial for your relationship right now.

1. **Weekly or Monthly Check-Ins:** Set aside a regular time to sit down and talk with your partner about how your relationship is going, any issues or concerns you may have, and what you can do to support each other.
2. **Relationship Goal Check-Ins:** Discuss your relationship goals and aspirations to see if you are both on track and if any adjustments need to be made.
3. **Emotional Check-Ins:** Ask each other how you are feeling emotionally and offer support and validation.
4. **Intimacy Check-Ins:** Discuss your physical and emotional intimacy, including any desires or concerns, and work together to ensure you both feel fulfilled and satisfied.
5. **Conflict Resolution Check-Ins:** Discuss how you handle conflicts and disagreements in your

relationship, and work together to find ways to improve communication and resolve disputes healthily and productively.

6. **Appreciation Check-Ins:** Make time to express gratitude and appreciation for your partner and the positive aspects of your relationship. This practice can help to build trust and strengthen your connection.

Important: Do not just spring relationship check-ins on your partner. Doing so might make them feel like they are being ambushed. Also, not everyone is comfortable or used to discussing their emotions. As such, it is vital to *pre-discuss* relationship check-ins.

First, discuss the concept of relationship check-ins with your partner. After they understand their purpose, communicate the need to schedule one in your calendars. Remember to set a mutually acceptable time and location and stick to it! Consider regular check-in dates as sacred, unbreakable appointments.

Important: **Relationship check-ins are safe spaces**. These conversations are not opportunities to fight or argue; they are a time for connection. Be honest with each other during these moments, but if something unpleasant arises, deal with the problem, not the person.

Alright! You have scheduled your relationship check-in; now what? Here are some questions to jumpstart ideas.

(Remember, focus on your relationship, not the kids, work, family members, etc.)

1. *"What happened to you this week, babe? Anything to share?"*
2. *"What was the worst/best thing that happened to you this month?"*
3. *"I thought I saw you looking unhappy during [event]. Was I right? Care to share?"*
4. *"Are you happy?"*
5. *"Do you feel I appreciate you enough?"*
6. *"We missed date night last week. Shall we schedule another one for this week? What are you in the mood for?"*
7. *"What do you think we can improve on in our relationship?"*
8. *"What are your thoughts about our sex life?"*
9. *"I know talking about feelings is new/difficult/alien to you. So, THANK YOU, babe, for getting out of your comfort zone for our relationship. Is there anything you want to add or change regarding our relationship check-ins?"*
10. *"Hey, how about we try something new, something we have never done before. What do you think? Any ideas?"*
11. *"What do you need?"*
12. *"How can I help?"*

THE POWER OF VULNERABILITY

The word "vulnerable" comes from the Latin word *vulnera-bilis*, which means "wounding." This, in turn, is derived from the Latin word *vulnerare*, which means "to wound." In modern usage, vulnerability refers to being open to harm or hurt (a chance to be wounded), either physically or emotionally. So, being vulnerable is difficult because it is not just about being honest. There is a risk because you are opening yourself up to possible pain.

For example, not everyone is comfortable with saying things such as:

"I feel hurt" (because it reveals you acknowledge that your partner has the power to hurt you)

"I'm sorry" (because it means you made a mistake or caused your partner hurt or pain)

"I'm scared" (because it could mean you are unsure or lost and do not know what to do)

Also, what if you say such things and your partner does not give you the necessary assurances? That can be another level of hurt. So being vulnerable is not easy because what you are really sharing is this: your weaknesses.

However, rebuilding trust and safety means showing up as your authentic self (strengths + weaknesses). So you must overcome any fears about revealing your flaws and limits.

One tip is to stop seeing vulnerability as a sign of weakness and start seeing it as a sign of strength. It is easy to say things such as, *"I make people smile," "I'm trustworthy,"* or *"I'm good at what I do,"* but it takes enormous courage and self-awareness to say something like, *"I'm falling apart," I don't know what I'm doing," "I'm afraid to lose you,"* and other similar things.

So, allow yourself to be vulnerable. Let your partner get to know the REAL YOU. It will deepen your bond because you have let them in. It also invites honesty. If you are willing to share your less-than-desirable traits, it will encourage your partner to share theirs.

Vulnerability also promotes a deeper understanding of each other. My friend Mavy[1] told me that she and her partner used to have arguments about leftovers all the time. She thinks he wastes food because he throws leftovers away. He told her he gets irritated with the "101 small containers in the fridge" that are either blocking something or falling and spilling all over the fridge. She eventually told him about a time in her childhood when her family went through poverty and that even one hardboiled egg was cherished. *"I was crying as I told him that. Remembering those moments is extremely painful, so I preferred to keep them in. I also didn't want him to look down on me or my parents. When I told him about it, he had nothing but compassion. He said he now understands this is more than just about leftovers. His ready kindness moved me, so I told him I would reduce the containers in the fridge. LOL."*

So, are you ready to be more vulnerable in your relationship? Here are some tips to think about.

1. Recognize your fears. Understand the fears or concerns holding you back from being vulnerable with your partner.

Examples:

I'm afraid they will start to look down on me.

I don't want to be rejected.

I've been betrayed before; I don't want to be betrayed again.

I don't want my partner to be disappointed in me.

2. Take baby steps. Start by sharing small things about yourself, gradually building to more personal and intimate topics.

Examples:

"I know I haven't been very open, but I want to change that and be more open with you."

"I've never shared this before, and you'll probably laugh, but I need to sleep with the lights on when you're away."

"There's been something on my mind lately, and I hope you can hear me out. I don't like having uninvited friends over. It stresses me out."

3. Practice self-compassion. Be kind to yourself as you work through your fears and vulnerabilities. Remember that

(1) EVERYBODY has fears and flaws, and (2) it takes strength to be vulnerable.

4. Practice self-forgiveness. If you want to share a past but serious mistake or wrongdoing that has shaped your thoughts, feelings, and actions now, learn to forgive yourself before sharing. Release yourself from the burden of guilt or shame and accept that you cannot change the past. All you can do is apply what you learned today and tomorrow.

5. Yes, it's about you. Vulnerability is about you. So, express *your* feelings and thoughts, fears and flaws, dreams and goals. Do not shift any responsibility to your partner. For example, do not say, *"If you had not cheated, I wouldn't be so insecure about our relationship."* Instead, say, *"I'm feeling really insecure right now, and I don't know how to handle it."*

6. Be honest. Be truthful and transparent about your feelings, even if they are difficult to express.

7. Trust your partner. Do not assume the worse in your partner. Believe that they will actively listen to you and respond with empathy and understanding.

8. Embrace imperfection. Recognize that vulnerability is not about being perfect. It is about being authentic and honest about your shortcomings.

9. This is a tip I learned from a couple who has been married for nearly 50 years: Ask for feedback on your behavior. Mary[2] told me that whenever she said or did something she was unsure of or was starting to regret, she asked her husband for his opinion. *"One time, I was annoyed with a friend and said 'No' to a big favor. I immediately regretted it, so I told my husband everything and asked, 'Am I being a bad friend here?' He said, 'Yes,' and proceeded to tell me why!"*

Before, I never asked my partner these kinds of questions. I wouldn't want to put myself under that much scrutiny, have my flaws pointed out, and be blamed for anything. Now, I know that is a sign of low self-esteem and a fear of vulnerability.

Needless to say, I'm not like that anymore and often ask my partner for feedback whenever I am unsure. Why? Because I trust him. I trusted him with my doubts and insecurities, knowing I would not be judged, but supported.

Trust and safety are essential for the health and longevity of your relationship. They are the basic foundations of any union, and without them, a relationship can become easily susceptible to hurt, pain, conflict, and even complete breakdowns. By rebuilding trust and safety between you, you can restore your relationship's sense of security and intimacy and create a strong, lasting bond.

In the next chapter, you will learn how to maintain a loving, supportive, and blame-free relationship. It will provide the information and skills you need to keep your relationship moving forward in the right direction.

9

LONG-TERM HEALTHY
COMMUNICATION MAINTENANCE

"The best way to predict your future is to create it."—

— *ABRAHAM LINCOLN*

R elationships require a lot of hard work. However, if
you can build a blame-free, supportive, and loving
one, you can be one of the world's happiest people. So, to
move forward positively, keep the following in mind.

5:1 AND 9/10

According to Dr. John Gottman, a recognized authority in the relationship niche, two statistics are prevalent in happy unions: **5 to 1** and **9 out of 10**.

People in stable, happy relationships have a **5:1 comple- ment-to-negative comment ratio**. For every complaint, there are five pleasant encounters between them. For exam- ple, they may get frustrated and say, *"Argh! Honey, I'm exas- perated you're late!"* but that single complaint is met with five or more positive statements such as *"Thank you," "I'm sorry," "You're looking great, babe," "You make me laugh so hard, you know that?" "Oh, thanks for thinking of me, honey,"* or *"How can I help?"*

On the other hand, people in toxic relationships communi- cate in a harmful way. Almost every statement is a critique or complaint, and compliments are scarce. And if a compli- ment "slips out," the other partner is so unused to hearing it that they may doubt the sincerity of the praise or conceive underlying motives for it (e.g., their partner wants some- thing in return, their partner is attempting to cover some- thing up, etc.).

Quick Question for You:

How do you assess your relationship right now in terms of 5:1? What is being expressed more often, compliments or complaints? If it's the latter, here are a few tips to help you shift to compliments.

1. Start the day with a compliment.

"Good morning, babe."
"Oh, forgot to thank you yesterday for ..."

2. For every complaint you want to say, think of at least three compliments you can say.

Complaint: dirty clothes are on the floor ... again
Compliments: they brought me flowers last week; they volunteered to get take-out before coming home so I don't have to cook; they always hold my hand

3. End the day with a compliment.

"Thanks, honey, for remembering to take out the trash. I always forget."
"Hmmm, you smell good."

Happy couples respond to their partner 9 times out of 10 when asked for attention. For example, when one says, *"Something is troubling me..."* or *"Why don't you come and sit down with me here for a minute,"* their partner will shift their attention to them 9 out of 10 times. Wanting attention from your partner is a natural part of a relationship because you want to feel loved, cared for, appreciated, seen, heard, and valued.

On the other hand, unhappy couples frequently reject their partner's calls for attention. Instead of seeing the request as an opportunity to connect, they are either uninterested or see it as selfish. For example, when one person attempts to tell the other about their day, the other "tunes out" and barely hears anything. The danger here is that not only is the opportunity to connect lost, but it also teaches the person seeking attention to stop asking for it and, as a result, stop sharing anything.

However, it is important to note that there is a difference between healthy and unhealthy attention-seeking behaviors. Healthy attention-seeking behaviors include expressing your needs and desires to your partner, sharing your thoughts and feelings, and engaging in activities together. On the other hand, unhealthy attention-seeking behaviors include manipulating your partner, using guilt or threats to get your way, and constantly seeking validation and reassurance.

Quick Question for You:

When was the last time you or your partner asked for attention? If you cannot remember, then it has been too long! If you need attention, don't be reluctant to ask for it.

Examples:

"Babe, got a minute to sit down and have some coffee with me?"

"I've been missing our quality time lately. It would be nice to plan something special for us to do together. What do you think?"

"Hey, can we talk for a bit?"

PASS PRAISE (NOT JUDGMENT)

Who doesn't like compliments? According to research, praise lifts the mood of both the giver and receiver of the compliment.[1] So, develop the habit of complimenting and praising your partner. (This also ensures you move toward the 5:1 ratio of happy couples above.)

Do not overthink this; something as simple as, *"Great job, babe!" "I knew you could do it!"* or *"Wow, honey, great meal!"* will do wonders. If you want to go further, try to be more specific when you praise your partner. For example, instead of saying, *"You're great,"* say, *"I love how you always put our family first."* Also, try to use "I" statements. For instance, instead of saying, *"You make me laugh,"* try saying, *"I appreciate how your sense of humor can turn my day around!"*

Also, compliments do not always have to be verbal. Here are some ideas; check one to try RIGHT NOW.

☐ Leave a sweet note for your partner.
☐ Send a text that says, "Thinking of you ♥" or "Thanks for the coffee/tea/breakfast this morning."
☐ Surprise them with a small gift like a favorite treat.
☐ Plan a special date night.

☐ Run an errand for them.

☐ Appreciate something they did. Offer a high five, thumbs up, wink, hug, kiss, smile, etc.

Important: DO NOT provide false praise; this elicits the opposite effect.[2] Instead of feeling great, your partner may think you are trying to manipulate them or want to get away with something. So, ensure that your compliments are always genuine and sincere.

If you are clueless as to what your partner wants to hear, some believe that women tend to prefer compliments about their appearances and personal qualities, such as their intelligence, kindness, and humor. For example, praise such as, *"You look great, honey,"* can make women feel attractive and secure in the relationship. Quality-related compliments such as *"I get slayed by your kindness, babe"* can make women think you see and understand who they are.

Men also appreciate these compliments but are more likely to value compliments on their abilities, accomplishments, and how they make women feel. For example, saying *"I believe in you"* is highly appreciated because it means you support them, making them believe they can accomplish anything. Praise such as *"I feel safe and secure with you"* appeals to a man's instinct to protect and provide. Men often feel a sense of responsibility to ensure the safety and security of their loved ones, and this praise reassures them that they are fulfilling that role.

However, the above are generalizations. You know your partner best, so express the kind of compliments you know they want to hear. If you are unsure about what type of compliment to convey, ask!

What do you do when you receive a compliment? There is nothing to express but appreciation (unless you believe the praise to be insincere). A simple *"Oh, thanks for noticing, honey"* is enough.

What if your partner is not comfortable with compliments? There are various reasons for this, but according to research, the foremost reason is low self-esteem.[3,4]

Building your partner's self-esteem is not your responsibility. However, you can influence them to be less self-critical. For example, begin with small compliments that are easy to accept, such as *"I appreciate the way you always make time for me"* or *"I like those new curtains you got. Great choice!"* Notice that these are "I" statements. Doing this makes it less likely for them to dispute your opinion.

You can also encourage your partner to practice self-care, whether it be through exercise, hobbies, or relaxation. This can help them feel better about themselves and be more receptive to compliments.

Additionally, you can motivate them to build mastery at something they already enjoy. For example, say your partner is a hobby cook, gardener, painter, photographer, etc. Encourage them to further their skills by surprising them with small gadgets or materials they need, talking about taking classes online or in person, and so on. Being great at something builds self-esteem and will thus make them more accepting of compliments.

TURN COMPLAINTS INTO REQUESTS

A healthy relationship is not devoid of problems. Whenever they occur, say what you want, not what you do not want. For example, instead of saying, *"Stop leaving dirty clothes on the floor!"* say, *"Babe, can you please put dirty clothes in the hamper from here on?"*

CREATE OPPORTUNITIES FOR SHARED EXPERIENCES

I went to Italy with some of my girlfriends a couple of years ago. One day, we took a trip to the Dolomite Mountains. While admiring the breathtaking views in front of me, I started to miss Greg terribly. I shared this with one of my friends, and she said, *"Do you know why you miss him so much now? It's because you want to share this moment. You know it will have even more meaning if you share it with him."* I immediately realized the truth in that statement and have since tried to create opportunities for shared experiences with my partner.

Sharing life experiences, especially ones neither of you has experienced before, builds a deep connection because you create a shared history. It fosters resilience and lays the groundwork for a relationship less prone to blame because there are too many good, shared times together.

Here are some ideas for you:

- □ weekend getaway to a place neither of you has been before
- □ impromptu lunch/coffee/dinner at a nearby place that just opened
- □ cook together, preferably something you have never eaten before
- □ start a new hobby together (e.g., walking, biking, painting, etc.)
- □ volunteer
- □ others:

_____

_____

_____

Important: Focus on the SHARING aspect of new experiences. Sometimes, things will go great; sometimes, not so much, which is okay too. Remember that the shared experience itself (the journey) matters, not the outcome.

ACCEPT YOUR DIFFERENCES AND FOCUS ON HOW YOU COMPLEMENT EACH OTHER

As we have discussed, blaming is subjecting your partner to your moral code, i.e., what you believe to be right or wrong.

But what about their moral code, their beliefs? Are they irrelevant? Of course not. So, release yourself from the fantasy that your partner should change and comply with you. No one is right, and no one is wrong; you two are just different. So, moving forward, focus on how your differences complement each other!

Here are some examples of differences complementing each other in a relationship:

1. One partner is spontaneous and impulsive, while the other is more cautious and thoughtful. Together, you can balance each other and make more informed decisions.
2. One partner is extroverted and outgoing, while the other is more introverted and reserved. Together, you can enjoy social events and also have quiet, intimate moments.
3. One partner is detail-oriented and organized, while the other is more relaxed and laid-back. Together, you can create a harmonious balance between structure and flexibility.
4. One partner is good at handling finances, while the other is good at planning and organizing household tasks. Together, you can create a strong foundation for your home and family.
5. One partner is adventurous and loves trying new things, while the other is more comfortable with routine and stability. Together, you can have exciting

experiences while also creating a stable and predictable environment.

6. One partner is a good listener, while the other is good at expressing themselves. Together, you can have meaningful conversations and deepen your emotional connection.

7. One partner is creative and artistic, while the other is analytical and logical. Together, you can solve problems in unique and innovative ways.

8. One partner is optimistic, while the other is more realistic and grounded. Together, you can balance hope and practicality and create a healthy outlook on life.

9. One partner is physically strong, while the other is emotionally strong. Together, you can support each other in different ways and overcome challenges as a team.

10. One partner is more experienced, while the other is younger and more naive. Together, you can learn from each other and grow as individuals and as a couple.

BE WILLING TO CONSTANTLY CHANGE

Yes, constantly. The goal is not to stay the same but to grow, improve, and evolve together.

Willingness to change can help prevent stagnation in the relationship and keep things fresh and exciting. When you are both open to trying new things and exploring new aspects of yourselves and your relationship, it can help prevent boredom and complacency from setting in.

Furthermore, change is an essential component of personal development. If you are willing to change, you are open to new experiences that may challenge your beliefs, attitudes, and actions. This can lead to self-discovery, personal growth, and a better knowledge of oneself and others.

Here is the great news: the fact that you have this book shows your willingness to change, and as you have read it, you have already been changing!

In conclusion, maintaining a blame-free relationship in the long term is essential for a healthy and happy relationship. It requires a shift—a change in your thoughts, emotions, and behavior in your relationship—for the better. By shifting your focus from fighting to mutual respect and understanding, collaboration, appreciation of differences, and committing to growing and evolving together, you WILL achieve a loving and long-lasting relationship for good.

SHARING ADVICE

As you begin to see positive shifts in your relationship, it's natural that you'll want to help others who are struggling – and there's an easy way you can do that right now!

Simply by sharing your honest opinion of this book and a little of your own experience, you'll show new readers where they can find the guidance they need to get their relationship back on track.

WANT TO HELP OTHERS?

Thank you so much for your support. It truly means the world to me.

Scan the QR code for a quick review!

CONCLUSION

"The best thing to hold onto in life is each other."

— *AUDREY HEPBURN*

There is no such thing as a conflict-free relationship. The problem arises when two people cannot connect and resolve the conflict but revert to hurtful and harmful words and actions. If you and your partner have been engaging more in the latter, it does not mean it's too late. In fact, research shows that *overcoming* relationship communication problems strengthens your bond with your loved one, promoting relationship stability and success.[1,2]

As I mentioned at the start, I have never been happier in my relationship than I am now. Of course, Greg and I did not just wake up knowing what we needed to do (if only we did!). We received A LOT of help and advice from counselors, happy couples in long-term relationships we knew, well-meaning family members and friends, and of course, our personal experience has revealed to us what works and what does not. I have just passed on this wealth of relationship knowledge to you.

Here is a quick recap of what we covered in this book to ensure you move from conflict to connection just as we have.

In Chapter 1: The Blame Game, you discovered how the dating phase might have set the stage for blaming in your relationship. You then learned what blaming really is, why you engage in it, and why you should stop it. This is also when you start to realize that while blaming points fingers at your partner, breaking free from it starts with YOU.

In Chapter 2: How to "Speak" to Improve Your Relationship, you learned that one of the main reasons you and your partner do not understand each other is that you might be using ineffective communication styles. You discovered that what you are NOT saying (non-verbal cues) may be more revealing, honest, and hurtful than the words you actually use. But perhaps one of the biggest shifts in this chapter for you is learning to communicate using "I" statements. So, please keep practicing this one!

In Chapter 3: Mastering Empathy in Communication, you found out how empathy, the ability to understand and share the feelings of your partner, opens the doors to deep understanding and connection. In fighting and blaming, you see your partner's faults; with empathy, you understand their WHY.

Arguing and resorting to blaming tactics is often a knee-jerk emotional reaction. You feel a strong emotion, and your way of coping is to blame somebody else for it. This is why in Chapter 4: Communicating with Emotional Intelligence, you discovered the importance of increasing your emotional intelligence. By taking a step back (mindfulness) and building self-awareness, you can process and manage your emotions effectively, decreasing the risk of reacting based purely on emotions.

Being in touch with and responsible for your emotions is one thing; expressing them is another. This is why, in Chapter 5: How to Communicate Your Emotions, you learned how to understand and label your emotions and express them effectively to fulfill your wants and needs in your relationship.

In Chapter 6: Blame-Free Conflict Resolution, you moved on to tackling your relationship's conflicts. You learned the importance of saying "I'm Sorry" and how these two simple words can jumpstart personal and relationship healing. You also discovered the most common phrases you should NOT use during conflict resolution to ensure your conversations do not worsen.

They say patience is a virtue, and after reading Chapter 7: The Power of Patience, you realize just how accurate that statement is. Here you understand what happens to your brain when you are impatient and how it contributes to conflict escalation. You then discovered how to develop patience and maintain it during potentially heated arguments.

Unhealthy communication between partners damages relationships. That is why in In Chapter 8: Rebuilding Trust and Safety in Your Relationship, you are provided with the tools you need to start putting your relationship back together.

Finally, in Chapter 9: Long-Term Healthy Communication Maintenance, you learned how to ensure fighting, blaming, and other unhealthy ways of communication never rear their ugly heads again in your relationship. In this chapter, you completely move away from old thoughts and behaviors to new ones that ensure relationship success.

As odd as it sounds, when Greg and I started our relationship, we didn't think we needed to invest so much time "getting to know each other." We were in love, decided to build a family, and all our plans and thoughts were about the future. We didn't stop and think that we needed to continue to learn and understand each other's past and present selves. This misunderstanding and maybe even unacceptance of each other led to many conflicts, fights, headaches, and heartaches. We sunk into misery deeper every day, oblivious to the fact that we were holding the shovels that were burying us. Luckily, armed with what I shared in this book, we are now "on the other side." Conflict no longer rules our relationship; connection does.

So, my final advice to you is this: go over this book again, chapter by chapter. But please do not just "read," but absorb, believe, practice, and live it. If you do, a long-lasting, happy, and fulfilling relationship where you and your partner feel seen, understood, valued, loved, and respected is yours.

APPENDIX A

APPENDIX A

WORKSHEET: I

Here is a step-by-step exercise to practice using "I" statements in your relationship.

1. Identify a specific situation or behavior you want to address with your partner. For example, it could be something like, *"When you interrupt me while I'm talking, I feel frustrated and unheard."*

What situation or behavior would you like to discuss with your partner?

_____

_____

_____

2. Practice using "I" statements to express your feelings and needs related to the situation. Instead of blaming or accusing your partner, focus on communicating your experience using statements starting with "I." For example, you might say, *"I feel frustrated when I'm interrupted because it makes me feel like you're not really listening to me."*

Practice what you want to say:

_____

_____

_____

3. If possible, role-play the conversation with a trusted friend or family member. Practice using "I" statements to express your feelings and needs related to the situation, and imagine how your partner might respond. This can help you refine your approach and prepare for different scenarios.

4. Have a conversation with your partner. Use the "I" statements you practiced to express your feelings and needs related to the situation, and be open to listening to your partner's perspective. Remember to focus on your experience and avoid blaming or accusing your partner.

5. Reflect on the conversation and identify areas for improvement. After the conversation, take some time to reflect on what went well and what you could do differently next time. This can help you refine your communication skills and build a stronger relationship with your partner.

Encourage your partner to use "I" statements during your conversation. However, do not force it. Remember, you have been practicing, so your partner might not be used to this speaking style yet.

Remember that using "I" statements can be a powerful tool for improving communication and resolving conflicts in your relationship. You can learn to express your feelings and needs constructively, respectfully, and effectively with practice and patience.

WORKSHEET: HOW TO FORGIVE

Forgiveness is a personal choice. It is up to you whether to grant it or prefer to hold a grudge. However, while you may not be responsible for a past unpleasant event, you are partly responsible for its current impact on your relationship. As such, working on forgiveness in your relationship may be the best thing for you to do.

1. Write down the incident that caused the hurt.

Describe the situation that caused the hurt in as much detail as possible. This could include what happened, how you felt then, and how it affected your relationship.

Your answer:

_____

_____

_____

_____

_____

2. Identify your feelings.

Take time to identify the emotions you experienced during and after the incident. Are you angry, hurt, disappointed, frustrated, or betrayed?

Your answer:

_____

_____

_____

_____

_____

3. Acknowledge your role in the situation.

Reflect on your own behavior and actions during the incident. Did you contribute to the situation in any way? Is there anything you could have done differently?

Your answer:

_____
_____
_____
_____
_____

4. Consider your partner's perspective.

Try to understand your partner's point of view. What might have led them to behave the way they did? How might they be feeling now?

Your answer:

_____
_____
_____
_____
_____

5. Decide what you need to forgive.

What do you need from your partner to move forward? Do you need an apology, an acknowledgment of the hurt they caused you, or willingness to have a conversation about what happened?

Your answer:

_____
_____
_____
_____
_____

6. Release the hurt.

To improve your relationship and mental health, it is important to let go of the hurt and anger you have been holding onto. This can be done through various techniques, such as journaling, meditating, talking to a trusted friend or therapist, etc.

What method(s) will help you release your hurt?

_____
_____
_____
_____
_____

7. Set boundaries.

Forgiveness does not mean that you have to forget what happened or be okay with abusive or hurtful behavior. It is essential to set boundaries and communicate your needs in the relationship.

What DON'T you want to happen again? Write it down and talk to your partner about it.

_____

_____

_____

_____

_____

8. Practice forgiveness daily.

Forgiveness is a process that takes time and effort to cultivate. Commit to practicing forgiveness and treating others with compassion and kindness.

What/who did you forgive today?

Examples: the person who cut me off the line at the grocery store, the driver who honked too loudly, etc.

_____

_____

_____

_____

_____

To be a forgiving person takes practice. Be patient with yourself and others, and focus on healing and moving forward healthily.

QUIZ: COMMUNICATION STYLE
SELF-ASSESSMENT
QUESTIONNAIRE

Here is a 12-point questionnaire to help you discover your communication style in your relationship.

1. When you disagree with your partner, do you tend to:

> a. Avoid discussing the issue
> b. Confront them immediately
> c. Wait until you calm down to discuss the issue

2. When making plans with your partner, do you:

> a) Always defer to their wishes and desires
> b) Insist on having your way
> c) Try to find a compromise that works for both of you

3. When you're feeling upset or angry, do you:

    a) Bottle up your emotions and keep them to yourself
    b) Lash out and say hurtful things
    c) Communicate your feelings calmly and clearly

4. When your partner does something that annoys you, do you:

    a) Keep quiet and hope they'll stop
    b) Criticize or blame them for their behavior
    c) Tell them how their actions make you feel and work together to find a solution

5. When your partner shares something important with you, do you:

    a) Pretend to listen while your mind is elsewhere
    b) Interrupt and change the subject to something you find more interesting
    c) Listen attentively and ask questions to show you care

6. When you need something from your partner, do you:

    a) Hint at what you want without being direct
    b) Demand that they do what you ask immediately
    c) Ask respectfully and allow them to say no

7. When you're in a disagreement with your partner, do you:

   a) Shut down and stop communicating
   b) Yell and scream to get your point across
   c) Listen actively and seek to understand their
      perspective

8. When your partner is upset, do you:

a) Dismiss their emotions and tell them they're overreacting
b) Try to fix the problem for them without their input
c) Offer support and validate their feelings

9. When you want to make a decision with your partner, do you:

a) Let them make all the decisions for fear of making the
   wrong choice
b) Refuse to compromise and insist on your way
c) Work together to find a solution that works for both
   of you

10. When you've hurt your partner's feelings, do you:

   a) Ignore the issue and hope it will go away
   b) Make excuses for your behavior and refuse to
      apologize

   c) Acknowledge your mistake, take responsibility, and apologize sincerely

11. When your partner does something you don't like, do you:

   a) Hold a grudge and bring it up later
   b) Use the silent treatment to punish them
   c) Express your feelings and work together to find a solution

12. When you want to express affection to your partner, do you:

   a) Assume they already know how you feel and don't need to be reminded
   b) Go overboard with gestures and gifts
   c) Express your love and appreciation in a sincere and genuine way

Scoring: For each question, give yourself 1 point for answer a), 2 points for answer b), and 3 points for answer c). Add up your total score to determine your communication style in relationships:

12-20 Passive Communication Style: You may struggle to express yourself, advocate for your needs in your relationships, and avoid conflict and difficult conversations.

21-30 Aggressive or Manipulative Communication Style: You may prioritize your needs and desires over your partner's and use tactics such as criticism, blame, or control to get your way.

31-36 Assertive Communication Style: You can express yourself clearly and respectfully while considering your partner's feelings and perspectives.

Important: This questionnaire is not a diagnostic tool but intended solely for educational purposes. Your communication style is complex and can be influenced by various factors, including but not limited to your upbringing, cultural background, personality, and past experiences. The results of this quiz should not be used to make any assumptions or judgments about your personality or behavior. They should not be relied upon as a substitute for professional advice or counseling.

WORKSHEET: ACTIVE LISTENING

Active Listening entails paying close attention to and fully comprehending the speaker's words. This way, you'll be able to effectively receive and interpret your partner during conversations, avoiding misunderstandings and tension in your relationship.

Note: When performing this exercise for the first time, choose a neutral or noncontroversial topic. (e.g., favorite Netflix TV series, a favorite song, etc.). The idea is to thoroughly comprehend what the other person is saying rather than engage in a debate.

1. Choose a speaker. Find someone you can speak with, such as a friend, family member, or coworker.

Who's your speaker?

_____

2. Find the right time and place. Choose a quiet time and place where you will not be distracted. This way, you can concentrate on the conversation.

When and where are you going to have this conversation?

_____

3. Turn to face the speaker. Maintain eye contact with the person speaking to demonstrate your engagement and interest.

4. Listen without interruption. Let the other person completely finish their thoughts before responding. Avoid interrupting, interjecting, or finishing their sentences.

5. Show active interest. Display your attention by nodding, smiling, or providing verbal cues like *"Oh," "Okay,"* or *"Uh-huh."*

6. Repeat what you heard. Tell the speaker what you heard back to confirm you understood them correctly. For example, say, *"Let me make sure I understand. You said... because ..."*

7. **Clarify.** If you don't fully understand what the speaker said, ask them to explain. Say something like, *"I don't get it. Why do you ...?"*

8. **Provide feedback.** Show that you have been actively listening by giving comments and asking questions. For example, you might say, *"It sounds like you like that TV series because it's based on your favorite book. Am I correct?"*

9. **Recap.** Summarize what was said at the end of the conversation to ensure you have the same understanding.

Example: *"Okay, so it's a surprise birthday party for Jack with a BBQ theme. It's next Saturday at 4 PM, your place. Correct?"*

As with any new skill, active listening takes practice. So, do this exercise again with someone you know (and who knows what the activity is about), or apply it each time you are conversing with someone.

WORKSHEET: MINDFULNESS BREATHING

Mindful breathing helps you be present in the moment without trying to change or control anything. If your mind begins to wander as you do this exercise, gently bring your attention back to your breath without judgment.

1. Find a comfortable seated position with your feet flat on the floor and your hands resting on your thighs.
2. Take a deep breath in through your nose, filling your lungs with air.
3. Hold your breath for a few seconds, then exhale slowly through your mouth, releasing all the air from your lungs.
4. As you exhale, bring your attention to your breath. Notice the sensation of the air leaving your body, the

rise and fall of your chest, and the feeling of your lungs emptying.

5. Inhale slowly and deeply through your nose, and focus on the sensation of the air entering your body.

6. Hold your breath for a few seconds, and then exhale slowly through your mouth, again focusing on the sensation of the air leaving your body.

7. Repeat this breathing pattern for several minutes, focusing your attention on your breath and the present moment.

WORKSHEET: IDENTIFYING BOUNDARIES IN YOUR RELATIONSHIP

Before you can start communicating your boundaries, you must first know what they are. The worksheet below will help you figure out your needs and limits.

But before you do, **take some time to reflect on your values and beliefs**. What are the things that are most important to you in your relationship?

Think about an instance when your partner made you uncomfortable, frustrated, or upset. These are your *triggers*. Make a list of your triggers and think about how you can respond to them in a healthy way.

What kind of boundary do you want to set?

Below are different kinds of boundaries. What kind of boundaries would you like to communicate with your partner?

Type of Boundary	Unacceptable
Physical Boundary	Examples: too much PDA when out, kissing in public, etc.
Emotional Boundary	Examples: verbal abuse, being forced to talk when I am not ready, etc.
Time Boundary	Examples: having no time for myself, having no time for dating
Intellectual Boundary	Examples: no jokes about my culture or religion
Financial Boundary	Examples: not talking about our savings, buying really expensive items without discussing them first
Sexual Boundary	Examples: not wanting to do certain sexual acts, not wanting to have sex when my partner is intoxicated

If you have other boundaries you wish to add, please do so. Also, after you complete the above worksheet, take some time and reflect on them before you go and discuss them with your partner.

QUIZ: AM I IMPATIENT?

The following is an 8-point questionnaire to help you discover if you have issues with patience.

1. How do you react when things don't go as planned?

  a) I feel frustrated or angry.
  b) I feel disappointed but remain calm.
  c) I feel relieved to have a change of plans.

2. How do you react to delays or setbacks in your work or personal life?

  a) I feel a sense of urgency to resolve the situation
    quickly.
  b) I become anxious or stressed.
  c) I take a measured approach to problem-solving.

3. How do you communicate with others when you're feeling impatient?

a) I speak quickly or interrupt others when they're speaking.

b) I use an aggressive tone of voice or blame others for delays or setbacks.

c) I remain calm and listen to others' perspectives.

4. How do you react to mistakes or errors?

a) I become frustrated or angry with myself or others.

b) I take a more measured approach to problem-solving.

c) I am forgiving and move on quickly.

5. How do you manage stress and anxiety?

a) I find it difficult to relax or take a break when I'm feeling stressed.

b) I have healthy coping mechanisms that help me manage my emotions.

c) I rarely experience stress or anxiety.

6. What is your overall attitude toward time?

a) I feel like there's never enough time in the day.

b) I have a more balanced view of time as a resource that can be managed effectively.

c) I feel like time is abundant and never a concern.

7) How does impatience impact your relationships and daily life?

a) It causes conflicts with others.

b) It makes it difficult for me to enjoy the present moment.

c) It doesn't really negatively impact my life.

8. How important is it to you to develop greater patience?

a) Very important - I want to work on developing more patience.

b) Somewhat important - I'm interested in learning more about patience.

c) Not important - I'm happy with my current level of patience.

Once you have answered all of the questions, take a moment to reflect on your answers and consider what steps you could take to cultivate more patience in your life.

Scoring:

If you answered mostly "a" or "b" to the questions, it suggests that you struggle with impatience in your life. This may be causing conflicts in your relationships or making it difficult for you to enjoy the present moment. This could indicate that you would benefit from learning strategies to cultivate more patience, such as mindfulness practices or problem-solving skills.

If you answered mostly "c" to the questions, it suggests that you have a relatively balanced and patient approach to life. However, it is still possible that you experience impatience in certain situations or that it impacts your relationships in subtle ways. In this case, you may still benefit from exploring strategies to cultivate more patience, even if your experience of impatience is less pronounced.

Important: This self-assessment quiz is not a substitute for professional diagnosis or medical advice. The results are intended for informational purposes only and should not be relied upon as a diagnostic tool. If you have concerns about impatience or other mental health conditions, please consult a qualified healthcare professional for a proper diagnosis and treatment plan.

NOTES

1. THE BLAME GAME

1. Alicke, M. D. (2000). Culpable control and the psychology of blame. *Psychological Bulletin*, *126*(4), 556–574. https://doi.org/10.1037/0033-2909.126.4.556
2. Malle, B. F., Guglielmo, S., & Monroe, A. E. (2012). Moral, cognitive, and social: The nature of blame. *Social Thinking and Interpersonal Behavior*, 331–350. https://doi.org/10.4324/9780203139677-28
3. Jerabek, I., & Muoio, D. (2019). It Wasn't My Fault: New Study Looks At Why People Hate Admitting Mistakes. PsychTests AIM Inc.
4. Okimoto, T. G., Wenzel, M., & Hedrick, K. (2012). Refusing to apologize can have psychological benefits (and we issue no mea culpa for this research finding). *European Journal of Social Psychology*, *43*(1), 22–31. https://doi.org/10.1002/ejsp.1901
5. Bradbury, T. N., Fincham, F. D., & Beach, S. R. (2000). Research on the nature and determinants of marital satisfaction: A Decade in Review. *Journal of Marriage and Family*, *62*(4), 964–980. https://doi.org/10.1111/j.1741-3737.2000.00964.x
6. Gold, J., Sullivan, M. W., & Lewis, M. (2011). The relation between abuse and violent delinquency: The conversion of shame to blame in juvenile offenders. *Child Abuse & Neglect*, *35*(7), 459–467. https://doi.org/10.1016/j.chiabu.2011.02.007

2. HOW TO "SPEAK" TO IMPROVE YOUR RELATIONSHIP

1. Holt-Lunstad, J., Birmingham, W. A., & Light, K. C. (2008). Influence of a "warm touch" support enhancement intervention among married couples on ambulatory blood pressure, oxytocin, alpha amylase, and Cortisol. *Psychosomatic Medicine*, *70*(9), 976–985. https://doi.org/10.1097/psy.0b013e318187aef7

2. Korom, P. (2018). Newcomb (1961): The acquaintance process. *Schlüssel-werke Der Netzwerkforschung*, 437–440. https://doi.org/10.1007/978-3-658-21742-6_102

4. COMMUNICATING WITH EMOTIONAL INTELLIGENCE

1. Goleman, D. (1995). *Emotional Intelligence*. Bantam Books.
2. Brackett, M. A., Warner, R. M., & Bosco, J. S. (2005). Emotional intelligence and relationship quality among couples. *Personal Relationships*, *12*(2), 197–212. https://doi.org/10.1111/j.1350-4126.2005.00111.x
3. Bhalla, P., Sidhu, S., & Ali, I. S. S. (2019, April). Impact of Emotional Intelligence on Quality of Romantic Relationships: Review Research. Blue Eyes Intelligence Engineering & Sciences Publication.

5. HOW TO COMMUNICATE YOUR EMOTIONS

1. *Universal emotions*. Paul Ekman Group. (2022, November 5). Retrieved April 1, 2023, from https://www.paulekman.com/universal-emotions/
2. Karnilowic, H. R. (n.d.). *The emotion wheel: Purpose, definition, and uses*. The Berkeley Well-Being Institute. Retrieved April 1, 2023, from https://www.berkeleywellbeing.com/emotion-wheel.html

THE IMPORTANCE OF REFLECTION

1. Ecaldre, P. M. (2022, May 14). *50 best quotes about overcoming relationship problems*. Inspiring Tips. https://inspiringtips.com/best-quotes-overcoming-relationship-problems/

7. THE POWER OF PATIENCE

1. Arnsten, A. F. (2009). Stress signalling pathways that impair prefrontal cortex structure and function. *Nature Reviews Neuroscience, 10*(6), 410–422. https://doi.org/10.1038/nrn2648
2. Ressler, K. J. (2010). Amygdala activity, fear, and anxiety: Modulation by stress. *Biological Psychiatry, 67*(12), 1117–1119. https://doi.org/10.1016/j.biopsych.2010.04.027
3. Rosen, L. D., Mark Carrier, L., & Cheever, N. A. (2013). Facebook and texting made me do it: Media-induced task-switching while studying. *Computers in Human Behavior, 29*(3), 948–958. https://doi.org/10.1016/j.chb.2012.12.001
4. McSpadden, K. (2015, May 14). *Science: You now have a shorter attention span than a goldfish*. Time. https://time.com/3858309/attention-spans-goldfish/
5. Ward, C. (2020, June). *Is impatience causing you stress? - selecthealth.org*. SelectHealth. Retrieved May 1, 2023, from https://selecthealth.org/blog/2020/06/impatience-causing-you-stress
6. *Name changed for privacy.*
7. Jackson, S. E., Steptoe, A., & Wardle, J. (2015). The influence of partner's behavior on Health Behavior Change. *JAMA Internal Medicine, 175*(3), 385. https://doi.org/10.1001/jamainternmed.2014.7554
8. *Name changed for privacy.*
9. Linehan, M. M. (2015). *DBT Skills Training Manual*. The Guilford Press.

8. REBUILDING TRUST AND SAFETY IN YOUR RELATIONSHIP

1. *Name changed for privacy.*
2. *Name changed for privacy.*

9. LONG-TERM HEALTHY
COMMUNICATION MAINTENANCE

1. Boothby, E. J., & Bohns, V. K. (2020). Why a simple act of kindness is not as simple as it seems: Underestimating the positive impact of our compliments on others. *Personality and Social Psychology Bulletin, 47*(5), 826–840. https://doi.org/10.1177/0146167220949003
2. Blatchford, E. (2017, June 19). *Compliments are good for your health, but not if they're fake.* HuffPost. Retrieved May 1, 2023, from https://www.huffpost.com/archive/au/entry/compliments-are-good-for-your-health-but-not-if-theyre-fake_au_5cd357fae4b0acea94ff00cc
3. Kille, D. R., Eibach, R. P., Wood, J. V., & Holmes, J. G. (2017). Who can't take a compliment? the role of construal level and self-esteem in accepting positive feedback from close others. *Journal of Experimental Social Psychology, 68*, 40–49. https://doi.org/10.1016/j.jesp.2016.05.003
4. Marigold, D. C., Holmes, J. G., & Ross, M. (2007). More than words: Reframing compliments from Romantic Partners fosters security in low self-esteem individuals. *Journal of Personality and Social Psychology, 92*(2), 232–248. https://doi.org/10.1037/0022-3514.92.2.232

CONCLUSION

1. Karney, B. R., & Bradbury, T. N. (1995). The longitudinal course of marital quality and stability: A review of theory, methods, and research. *Psychological Bulletin, 118*(1), 3–34. https://doi.org/10.1037/0033-2909.118.1.3
2. Graber, E. C., Laurenceau, J.-P., Miga, E., Chango, J., & Coan, J. (2011). Conflict and love: Predicting newlywed marital outcomes from two interaction contexts. *Journal of Family Psychology, 25*(4), 541–550. https://doi.org/10.1037/a0024507

Made in the USA
Las Vegas, NV
14 November 2024

11818917R00115